HOW THIS BOOK WAS WRITTEN

Letter after letter Matteo shares his thoughts with me and I take dictation on the computer. It's an amazing experience to watch him write a book. As you can imagine, it takes a long time and this book is no exception. He began *Secrets* over one year ago and the following pages contain the fruits of our labor of love. Just to be clear, these are Matteo's own words without any editorial changes. My husband and I find it fascinating that Matteo never goes back and corrects anything - his thoughts always come out perfectly the first time. It is this way with all of his poetry as well, no matter how complicated the rules may be for different types of poems.

He starts by writing the table of contents and lays out what he wants to cover in the book. Then he's off and running. All we need is more hours in the day!

Matteo and I both hope you enjoy this book and that it provides some information and ideas you may find pertinent to your life and the life of your child, client or friend with autism. But most of all, we hope that it lifts you up and compounds feelings of hope, curiosity and wonder that you may already have toward this special population of people with whom we are blessed to be sharing our lives.

Blessings to you each day!

Annette and Matteo (and Dad, too!)

Matteo Musso/Over The Fence Publishing
P.O. Box 2227
Livermore, California 94551
www.matteomusso.com
matteo@matteomusso.com

Publisher's Note:
All brand names and product names used in
this book or trademarks, registered trademarks,
are trade names of their respective holders.

No warranty, express or implied, is delivered
by the author or publisher with respect to the
contents of this book.

Autism Secrets Revealed / Matteo Musso.
-- 1st ed.

ISBN 978-0-9988636-6-5

Autism Secrets Revealed

by
Matteo Musso

Love Works best
teo

Over The Fence Publishing
Livermore, California

Matteo's writings speak to the heart of what it means to be a compassionate human – taking our time to truly listen to those we care about. He has broken through the assumptions of others and through this, offers incredible lessons and insight enabling us to learn through his experiences.

Matteo continues to expand the possibilities of neuro-diverse understanding in a way that relates to each one of us.

~ Phil Didlake, MT/BC
(Music Therapist)

Mom and Dad,
I love you more than you
will ever know.

DEDICATION

I dedicate this book to all
of my loving grandparents:
Grandpa Frank, Grandma Lucia, Papa and Grandma Mary.
I also dedicate this book to my Great Aunt Lillian.

Your love for me and the support you all give
both here on Earth and from Heaven, is felt
in the depths of my heart. Without it,
I would not be writing this book today.
I love you forever.

Love,
Teo

CONTENTS

The Definition of Me

A lyric poem by Matteo Musso, Age 14
May 30, 2018

I Am:

A heart full of love and compassion.

A mind full of ideas and original thoughts.

A soul seeking clarity during this human existence.

A spirit sharing positive energy with those who
will accept it.

A teacher to those seeking deeper meanings of
life's daily experiences.

A guide for those seeking comfort during life's trials.

A teen wanting to inspire acceptance for all.

A voice for the silent ones.

A messenger sharing loving ideas from our Creator.

I am not defined by any disability with which I may be labeled. I am handicapped only by those who place limitations on me. What defines me comes from within my own heart and is accompanied by the self-esteem which develops as I grow and am exposed to love and nurturing education.

A Greeting from Matteo

I'm glad you're reading this book. Whereas autistic people vary from each other as much as NTs (neurotypicals), there are a few things I'm pretty sure we have in common and we'd like all of you to know. How do I know this? Because we connect with each other in special ways that NT's don't understand yet. But on a less "woo-hoo" note, I have proof and witnesses. Whenever I give a public talk where there are some autistics in the audience, they chime in with audible statements of support and agreement. My pre-verbal colleagues (those who have yet to master verbal speech) let loose their fun sounds of communication at the perfect times, right after I've said (spelled on my letterboard) one of my zingers. My speaking colleagues have even been known to jump out of their seats and say to everyone, "He's so right!" or "That's true!"

Or, another way they show their support and interest, is that they just stay awake during my presentation. Believe me, I think that says something! There was an autistic guy in his early 20's who was at one of my first talks in Minnesota in 2015. This one went on for two hours and he remained calmly in his seat the entire time. His parents told my mom afterwards, that was the first time he'd ever done that and they were so shocked. I liked having him in the audience, supporting me with his sounds at a decibel level

I could hear coming from him way in the back row. They sat back there because they anticipated having to leave at some point during my talk, but they didn't. He was happy to support me saying things to the audience for him, too.

So, I call these "my Secrets of Autism Revealed." Maybe you've assumed some of these ideas during your journey, but perhaps not in as much such depth as you'll read here. Or maybe your heart has been saying some of these things, but your brain isn't truly on board in a way that allows you to act on them. I know outside influences affect your decision-making when it comes to us, our therapies and capabilities, whether they be teachers, doctors, therapists, family, friends or books.

Well, I hope to be the biggest positive influence on you; the one that reminds you to listen to your heart and intuition when it comes to raising, teaching, interacting and just hanging out with us. Science tends to set limits on us and override your intuition sometimes. I'm going to lasso you now and invite you to open your mind and let in some first-hand information from someone who has over 131,400 hours of experience actually being autistic. Enjoy!

Happily yours,
Teo

IDEA 1

Brilliant Minds

Autistics are brilliant minds
trapped inside uncooperative bodies.

IDEA:

Autistics are brilliant minds
trapped inside uncooperative bodies.

MY MAIN POINT

We may have challenges getting our bodies to
obey, so we do things spontaneously or impul-
sively that are misinterpreted as " intentional
behavior."

MY TAKE

Our bodily actions are not always reflective of
our intentions in a given situation.

MY EVIDENCE

I watch my body do things sometimes, that I
did not give it instructions or permission to do!
It happens with my colleagues, too. Too often,
I feel like an observer at a Broadway play. It's a
very expensive ticket to get, as the acting is top
notch and professional. I convince others that
I am in control by the ease and grace with
which I do my "bodily actions." But here's the
secret...I'M OBSERVING JUST LIKE YOU! And
believe me, it's not always fun.

Here's a poem I wrote recently because hormone surges are making me crazy! It was written following a long meltdown.

A Tough Road
August 8, 2018

Don't turn left, turn right instead,
Neither of us knows what lies ahead.
Neither have been traveled on,
I hope it doesn't last for long.

The monster chases me all the time,
I usually am faster, but not this time.
I hesitated for an instant,
He took me captive in his prison.

I could not shake him, though I tried,
My brain got stuck, my heart just cried.
I lost control and hovered about,
Watching helpless from the cloud.

Mom was a trooper, to say the least,
And she did nothing to unleash the beast.
The schedule changed, the beast grabbed hold,
Of changes that remained untold.

I lost myself amidst the current
    That flowed downstream so fast.
Languishing in such turmoil and
    Feeling like I'm going to crash.

Out of control, no grounding there,
Was scary to say the least.
I saw myself turn instantly
From sweet young guy to beast.

Then Mom was done, she'd had enough
    And ran out of ideas.
She just laid down and hugged the pillow
    And then out came the tears.

Ironically, it happened then,
I found my way back home.
My body ached, the adrenaline gone,
And peace was mine to own.

Mom's tears were healing gifts from God,
Streaming down her face like rain.
And I knew then that we'd be fine,
And peace would rule again.

But does it have to be so strong,
This effect of surging hormones?
I pray the answer from God is "No,
The worst has passed, you're victorious."

I pray that Mom and Dad remain
    Firmly on my side,
And that they choose to know for sure
    Their loving boy's still inside.

To my body: Please adhere to my pleas and respect
my family who loves me so. I love them more than
words can express.

There's a whole other book there regarding puberty and the non-verbal autistic, but that's for later. Back to our independently-thinking bodies...

A colleague of mine burst out of an RPM (Rapid Prompting Method – the teaching method I use to communicate) session a couple of years ago. I was in the lobby waiting for my next RPM session when a large blur caught my eye. I wouldn't find out what it was until later. Then I saw my RPM teacher, Lenae, running down that same hallway waving a letterboard. She wasn't as fast as "the blur," so I recognized her. Then another lady came running out with a panicked look on her face. They both wanted to catch up with that blur, for sure! A few minutes later, the mystery of "the blur" was solved. The two ladies were walking calmly back toward the RPM office with the fastest RPM student in history. After he was seated again and ready to work, he told Lenae and his mom that it was as if his head was floating above his body as it ran down the hall. He could not feel his physical body at all, nor could he control it. Another convincing Broadway actor!

Another struggle I have regarding bodily actions is that OCD (Obsessive Compulsive Disorder) takes over, hence the "getting stuck." The actions range from stuff like nose-picking to pacing (guess which is Mom's favorite?) and lots in between. Only to be topped by my repeating a suggestion or observation I have

("Let's go to dinner, let's go to dinner, let's go to dinner," or "That's Mom's water, that's Mom's water, that's Mom's water") or sharing the plans I have for the next few seconds (after I get the appropriate response from someone who knows it!), "The song is over, it's over, it's over, next one, next one, next one." Now, even if you respond with the expected response, depending on how stuck I am, there's no guarantee that will even work. I'll give helpful suggestions below though, don't worry.

I hear myself saying these things over and over, and I guess until I hear a response, it's like it's an incomplete sentence – and I'm a guy who likes completing things in life. Don't leave me hangin' here, guys! Do I like this? No. Do I mean to drive you nuts? No. Would I like to learn how to control this and get unstuck? Heck, yes! We're working on these mysterious conundrums in our house. I'll keep you posted.

Hint 1

Please be aware that not all bodily actions are behavioral.

Apply consequences only sparingly. Take time to learn how to distinguish between a true behavior and a bodily action. Behaviors are done with a goal in mind; either to get something we want or to express disagreement with a decision you made. I, of course, have no behaviors (ha), so Mom and Dad live on "Easy Street" regarding these decisions.

A bodily action doesn't have a *sane* goal that you could identify.

Then enters that bewildering middle-ground; bodily actions that do result in us getting or accomplishing something, but which are impulsive. They happen so fast and then they're over before we know it. They require a trigger, either internal or external. For example, I could be in an RPM session and have a thought enter my mind, like, "I should put that coffee cup in the sink!" Off I go, down the hall to the kitchen to accomplish that task. Mom, Sara or Lenae (the people I do RPM with) wouldn't even know what hit them.

My friend takes glasses off of other people (and it's not one of his most popular impulses with strangers). My other friend can do a twisty move, escaping from someone's grasp and be in our pantry grabbing crackers and shoving them in his mouth before you can say, "Boo." I must say I admire that about him!

Another trigger for me is food. Cooking it, eating and shopping for it...I like it all. I even like cleaning up after I help prepare it. I get obsessed with other people eating their own food, too. Sometimes I just want them to finish that last bite or last sip. I inspire them by saying, "Finish it," over and over. Again, the need to finish what was started. Weight Watchers wouldn't hire me!

Back to my "Hint 1," punishments/consequences only help me punish myself psychologically. Thankfully Mom and Dad know that, but some forms of therapy do not. We don't do those therapies anymore, thank God!

Hint 2

Redirect.

Redirecting can be helpful if done immediately and in a relaxed way. The more times I'm allowed to say something, the deeper the hole becomes. If I'm using a shovel and the repeated statement is the dirt, if I'm left alone to repeat and repeat, soon that hole will become deeper than I am tall. That's when panic sets in. That's when an OCD loop can turn into a major meltdown. The trick is redirecting us in a "chill" way, not out of your fear of the potential meltdown or the frustration you may feel by us driving you crazy.

Here are some ideas:

1. Have a squishy thing available for us to hold, or clay to mold. Help us feel our body. Compressions at this particular time do not work for me. You'd be invading my energy space.

2. Mom will say, "Incoming!" to get my attention, then gently throw a ball to me. I have no choice but to focus on the ball. Make sure to get the person's attention first, though.

3. Write on a piece of paper, a self-directing statement for us to read, either out loud or to ourselves (yes, they know how to read even if

they can't prove it to you...trust me!). "TEO, STOP SAYING 'FINISH IT, MOM.'" Then just point to it next time we say it out loud and have a smile on your face and in your heart. KNOW that it will work. (That's a big step. More on that later.) It may take some practice because it's new, but it is effective. Lenae and Soma (the founder of RPM) discovered this technique. Mom has been using it recently and I find it refreshing and useful.

4. Reassuring us that you will finish the food (or whatever the statement is about) in a specific amount of time or after a different activity is helpful. Example: "Teo, I'll finish my water after I get off the treadmill. I really need to save it for now because I'll be thirsty later." The explanation will work for some if it's done at the beginning, prior to all of our logic and reasoning skills disappearing into the Black Hole of OCD. If you never intend to "finish it" say that, but calmly explain why, just once though. Don't you start repeating yourself, too! Throwing it away while we're watching, would probably be a dire mistake. I know I went ballistic when Mom experimented with that in an effort to eliminate the object of my OCD obsession from my line of sight. Rookie mistake! I mean, hey, it might work for you, but it was really hard on me emotionally. Try saying something like, "I'll just have Dad cover it up with a paper towel so it won't trigger you anymore." Or try having the person, the autist, face another direction –

sit somewhere else or do an activity out of the room if you can get them to move, then move the offending item

Hint 3

You may not think your child has OCD, but they easily could!

What is repeating something over and over again, anyway? Is it autism or is it OCD? Well, what's in a name? Just know that if it brings us pleasure and comfort (like flapping our hands in front of our eyes), it's a stim and a cool, creative part of our autism. We've figured out a harmless way to soothe ourselves. Don't stop us, by the way (please read my first book, *Handbook of Us*, for more on this). You soothe yourselves, in your own way I've noticed, by biting your nails, twirling your hair or tapping your foot on the floor under the table. But, if you see our energy shifting or our heart rate increasing, you'll know it's OCD taking over our brains. Believe me, if we could stop it ourselves, we would!

Hint 4

Meditation for grounding.

Even if this is way outside your "norm" for the day, please consider it for your autistic friend. I had to introduce my mom to the idea. (I'll address it more in Idea #10.) Whether you believe it will help or not, it certainly can't hurt! Remember that we live different lives than you and we experience every sight, sound, feeling and movement differently in our bodies than you. Please give it a try. The reason we lose control of our bodies in the first place is that we are not grounded. You'll want to get meditations from a source you trust because they are powerful. I highly recommend those from my friend and Master Shafaw healer, Behrooz Danadoost. The website is: www.ehealing.org and it has some great meditations you can download.

Hint 5

Stay calm yourself.

I'll talk in depth about this in *Idea 8*, but for now, just know that we are mirror images of you – all kids are, as a matter of fact. If you get frustrated guess what, so will we. If you get mad guess what, so will we. If you get disappointed guess what, so will we. But if we're non-verbal we'll just internalize it and that's even harder. Learn to take deep breaths (oh...and here's my chance to encourage you to meditate!).

IDEA 2

We Understand

We understand everything you say.

IDEA:
We understand everything you say.

MY MAIN POINT

Speak in age-appropriate voices and vocabulary to communicate with us.

MY TAKE

Do you believe this? That we truly understand everything you say? From my experience, I'd say the majority of people in society do not.

MY EVIDENCE

Why do I say this? Because so many people I have encountered speak to me differently than they do to others. Whether it's slower speech, use of simple vocabulary, talking in a louder volume or my favorite, speaking in partial sentences. And finally, people would so often talk about me as if I wasn't standing right there with them, but I was!

Hint 1

Slower speech can be confusing to me because speech has a rhythm to it.

When it's slowed down too much, it's less recognizable. It would be like playing your favorite song at a fraction of its normal speed. You're used to hearing all the notes together but if they were so spread-out, I bet you'd have a hard time recognizing that favorite tune of yours. Temple Grandin told me once (actually twice, on two separate occasions), that she has a hard time understanding me when I communicate by spelling my thoughts because Mom is calling out one letter at a time. She has to stop listening and wait until Mom says the whole word or phrase. Then it's easier for her to understand. Again, sometimes getting components separately is more challenging than receiving the whole, in a timely manner.

Hint 2

Constructing special phrases just for us, consisting of words that have a syllable count of four or less and are limited to those words found in large print children's books is not necessary.

Also, please keep in mind that speaking in partial sentences is funny-sounding. When you speak to the person standing next to me in full and complete sentences, including all the little words and phrases, feel free to carry on in the same manner when addressing us. We can handle it. Remember that we're still mirrors of you in this regard, too. If you want us to learn to speak in choppy sentences, speak to us in choppy sentences. But if you'd like us to speak intelligibly, please do so to us so we have proper models to emulate. Ex: "Teo, want apple or pear?" vs. "Hey Teo, would you like an apple or a pear for a snack?"

It's harder for you! You really don't have to think so hard and create a language of "simplicity" for us because that's not always what it is, despite the best intentions of those giving this advice. Just talk to us as if we're your friend and we're sitting at Starbucks. It will make life better for all of us.

Hint 3

Speaking in a louder volume...

Well, that helps my grandma when she doesn't wear her hearing aids, but it doesn't help me. In fact, it's a bit harder to process the words. I have to cover my ears because the vibrations are stronger. When I do that, people usually get the hint at least for a minute or two. "Loud talkers" will unknowingly let their volume creep back up but I can handle the vocal crescendo. It's the strong, shocking, sudden accents that get to me. So no, talking louder is not helpful, at least to me.

Hint 4

Please acknowledge us in conversation.

The worst of all is when people talk about me or speak for me like I'm not there, when in reality, I'm standing with or pacing close by them. So, if you're going to speak about your autistic friend while they're standing right next to you or even if they're in the vicinity, please acknowledge them by saying something like, "Hey Jimmy, I know you hear and understand this conversation, but I thought I'd just tell your teacher what happened last night." That shows us respect and teaches others how to be respectful of non-verbals.

Consider for a moment, how you think of someone in a wheelchair or someone who is blind. I'm asking you to put autism in a category with other special ways of living (I don't like the word "disability"), forgetting anything you've heard or read about the intellectual limitations of autistic people. It's a real-life change to put this into action, "Don't judge a book by its cover."

IDEA 3

Eye Contact and Speech

Eye contact and speech have no effect
on listening and understanding.

IDEA:
Eye contact and speech have no effect on listening and understanding.

MY MAIN POINT

They're using different parts of the brain and different learning channels.

MY TAKE

People could easily understand this by taking a neurology class (haha).

MY EVIDENCE

Eye contact requires muscle control, integration of primitive reflexes (thank you Dr. Masgutova!) and an ability to process information through visual learning channels (thank you Soma!) which may or may not be available to us at any given time during the day.

Hint 1

Speech has its own neuro-pathways
to forge.

Comprehension and speech, although both processed on the left side of the brain, use different areas of it. They are as different as the concepts of hearing and listening. If one can hear and chooses to listen, then they most likely understand. Analyzing a statement is not the same as being able to say a statement with speech. So, to say that an autistic person doesn't comprehend what you say because he/she can't repeat it back to you, or write an answer down (motor skill required), is crazy, excuse my French. Why would people choose to assume that? Why do they lump those things together?

Here's an example: Mom thought I didn't understand the concept of addition because I didn't consistently give her the right answer to single digit addition problems. She'd tell Dad, "He doesn't get the concept of adding two groups of stuff together to get a whole bunch more stuff." I just had to let that statement go because I had no way of defending my intelligence. The truth is that I was bored out of my mind and had to find ways to entertain myself. Staring off and watching Lion King or Cinderella in my mind were two of my entertainment favorites. I still love those movies!

Hint 2

Understanding Speech

If eye contact and speech were mutually required for us to understand the spoken word, you couldn't call for your husband to bring you coffee in bed (located in your room in the back of the house), as he sat watching his morning sports show in the living room, right? If eye contact was necessary, how could he understand what you wanted unless he has the power to see through walls? Why is it different for us?

Now mind you, it's perfectly plausible that we understand what you want us to do at any given time, as you ask us with verbal direction, but we can't make our body comply. But you see, that's a totally different issue. One of the biggest challenges of autism is our uncooperative bodies. Sometimes they do impulsive actions without permission.

For example, Mom can ask me to take dirty clothes to the laundry room. I understand her request, even if she's being a bit boisterous from the other room but I can have a hard time getting my body to start the action. If I'm trying to do it and it's not working, I begin my anxiety voyage due to frustration. Guess what; then comes the OCD and that can lead to major meltdowns. No one wants that, trust me! A gentle touch on my body from a helper can prevent this escalation, as I can feel my body connected to this Earth, once again. Then I'm off and running with the task.

If there's a pile of clothes on my bed and Mom wants me to hang them up (this often happens), she may need to hang up the first item with me, then my brain-body connection remembers.

It's that simple, but only if you understand this is the issue. It's not that I didn't comprehend the directive from Mom, it's that I got "stuck" and simply couldn't comply without her help for a second. Eye contact had nothing to do with it. It's not just me who wishes you to know this. My autistic friends are playing the same tune on their letterboards or other means of communication. For others to realize this, especially Mom and Dad, means the world to me (us) and creates a deeper bond and mutual respect.

By the way, never, ever, ever grab your child's chin and turn their head toward someone you want them to look at. We'll fight you tooth and nail on that one! It's so demeaning and makes us feel like we're dogs on one of those gentle-leader leashes (leashes that go on a dog's nose instead of around their neck). If we don't look, it's because we can't for any number of reasons. Your hands on our faces will only do harm, demean us and hurt your relationship with your child or autistic friend. Sorry to be so blunt, but it's serious information for me to share.

What if you turned in a report to your boss and he/she suddenly appeared in your office and slammed that report down on your desk. Then, he/she put his hand behind your head and pushed it down toward that report until your nose was two inches from it while saying, "Look at that! I can't believe you wrote that!" How-would you feel? I'm really adamant about this one, can you tell? I see it done way too much so I have to stick up for my non-verbal colleagues here. If you're one who does this, I know your intent is not like that of the boss in my analogy, but it's the only way I could think of to get my point across in a way perhaps, that you can relate. If someone is saying good-bye to your child and you want to teach them to respond somehow, do it gently and respectfully please. You could raise their hand in a soft waving motion, but better yet, you could say to that person, "He'd say good-bye if he could. He's sure thinking it." Thanks for listening to this one. We all really appreciate it!

IDEA 4

Different Experiences

Everyone experiences life differently.

Being Autistic

By Matteo Musso

Being autistic is not what it seems.
It's just like being wrapped up in your dreams.
Not all you control, sometimes feels like a movie,
With someone playing you in each scene.

I watched him, that teen making "Martian" sounds
with his voice. I observed his ways and compared
them to those of others.

He skipped down the produce aisle on the
way to get kale...they stared.

Sounds escaped his mouth as he enjoyed modern
art at a museum...they judged.

He didn't say "hi" or look at them...
they were hurt.

He didn't embrace them long enough...
they wondered if he loved them.

I watched him, that teen, and saw strength, self-
expression, bravery and unimaginable patience.
But most of all, I saw love expressed in unique ways.

Did they feel it?

IDEA:
Everyone experiences life differently.

MY MAIN POINT

Autistics may be different than the majority of people in some big ways, but we are also more like you than you think.

MY TAKE

We are stereotyped by much of society in many ways due to lack of education and information about what it's really like to "live autistic." Some stereotypes might include:

- We have a low IQ
- We don't understand language
- We're defiant
- We have bad behavior
- We choose to ignore you
- We're rude or unfriendly
- We're "inappropriate"
- We're simpletons
- We're limited in what we can learn
- We like being alone and don't care about having friends
- We're very pushy and spoiled

There are plenty more but you get my drift.

MY EVIDENCE

Well, I'm a professional listener and a sociologist, cultural and social anthropologist, of sorts. I've got a good 15 years of this studying under my belt!

Hint 1

Changing your perscpective
changes everything!

Take it from someone who's been on the receiving end of these societal misunderstadings. I have had to learn patience way beyond your understanding (no offense).

If you can, please re-read the previous list and consider if you've ever felt this way or thought these things about someone in your life. First, reflect on autistic people that you know. Now here is the same list but viewed from the opposite perspective...

- We have high IQ's
- We understand language
- We're trying our best to comply
- We don't necessarily have "bad behavior." It's that our bodies do their own actions sometimes without our permission (or out of habit).
- We'd never choose to ignore you. (Sensory input around us or inside of us may just be too much to bear at any given moment.)
- We're kind and would love to be able to be outwardly friendly if we could
- We're not "inappropriate." We just need to do things sometimes to soothe ourselves from our challenges in this world.
- We're very complex people and we'd love to be challenged intellectually.

- Our ability to learn things knows no limits. Limits are imposed on us by others.
- Regarding friends, we love them as much as you do. We're all different from each other in this way – just as you NTs are.
- We're not "pushy" or "spoiled." We're just getting our intense needs me so we can assimilate into this world.

Now, the fun one. Reflect on people you don't know; someone you've seen at Target or the grocery store. Maybe a kid was acting "obnoxious" by first glance but was really autistic instead? Can this new checklist reside in the forefront of your brain storage? Next time, say a silent, "I know," to the child with a compassionate smile. Shoot one toward the mom or dad, too. You'll make their day! We're like everyone else who just wants to be understood.

Hint 2

You can feel free to approach us, even if we can't speak with you.

People often ask Mom how to approach me or if they can give me a hug. I'd like to invite you to treat us the same as you do others. Unless, that is, you're a loud talker (as previously discussed), stand too close to people and generally invade their space, are the "Energizer Bunny" or caffeine-high guy, or if you walk up to people and give attack-hugs when people aren't ready. If you are one of these people, then yes, please back it off about 50% for us. (I say this with love, but we may not be alone here with this request.)

Hint 3

Hugs.

Hugs deserve their own paragraph. Many people love them but there are also many who aren't really huggers. Some hug only those they're close to while others hug anyone they meet. We're as different in this regard as you NTs are, but then add in our human energy sensitivities. My advice is to think back to toddlers prior to their language acquisition. I've watched Mom with my nieces and nephew. She gets down to their level and extends her arms with a non-verbal invitation for them to jump in there. Most of the time they do, but if they don't, she doesn't let her heart sink or take it personally. They seek her out later, I've noticed. That's because little kids are extra sensitive to human energy, too. We're all born with this innate skill, but we are taught things as we grow that tend to bury this gift.

So try treating us like this regarding hugs. Oh, and try not to make us hug people out of obligation or out of social convention, it's stressful. I bet most people would enjoy fewer heart-driven hugs than tons of surface ones.

Hint 4

Practice makes perfect!

We're like NTs in that way, too. We're capable of learning anything that we're taught if given ample practice. In some cases it may require the discipline of an olympic athlete in training to accomplish a task that comes easy to most. But hey, Steph Curry didn't wake up one morning with the ability to shoot so many three-pointers for the Warriors; he had to practice and have a knowledgeable coach to teach him.

IDEA 5

Autism is Not a Disorder

Autism is not a disorder but rather,
a spiritual energy.

IDEA:
Autism is not a disorder but rather,
a spiritual energy.

MY MAIN POINT

Why is autism called a "disability?"

MY TAKE

Some challenges within the autism label may be debilitating, but let's remember to call an apple an apple, not an orange. If our tummies hurt, that could be caused by many things, but it's not autism. If we make strange sounds, is it autism or a release of energy? If we do repetitive activities, are they a brilliant calming mechanism or autism? What if autism describes only the way we can access and use our senses and different parts of our brains? Would autism still be a "disability," or would it become a desirable trait that many NTs would want to have?

I was doing a talk once to a bunch of sixth graders and one of them asked me, "Will you ever 'get over' your autism?" I did the politician-thing and answered that question with my own question to him: "If I overcome my challenges but keep my gifts of math, understanding physics, visualizing art, seeing colors with music, tasting food with intense imagery and some other fun things I can do, will I still be autistic?" I'm not going to answer that one; it's thrown out there for all of you.

MY EVIDENCE

If autism were merely a "disorder," and not a spiritual energy, how are we able to sense the truth of your hearts so much then? Why do so many of us know things we've never been taught? Why are our neurological systems functioning differently than most? No matter the medical cause or explanation, there is a reason for this and God (Universe, whatever you believe) made it so. Open your mind to see other ways of existing on this planet. We have no disorder. We are a different type of spiritual being trying to figure out how to thrive in this world, that's all. If we were just like everyone else, we'd be just like everyone else. Profound, huh? Maybe the tortures of this world's sensory circus force us into our own world so we can refine our spiritual skills. Then we can reappear somehow, and share our ideas with you or even remind you of things you've forgotten.

Hint 1

We all reappear!

Some of us with typing, some with letterboarding, some with speech and still others with refined pantomime skills. What you get to see is up to you, God and your autistic friend. I know you would probably like to be solely in charge of this, but I'm afraid that's not how it works.

Hint 2

Be open to discussing spirituality
with your autistic friend.

Many of my colleagues on the spectrum are full of ideas and experiences regarding this topic. If they do choose to share these things with you, please do not judge their experiences. Many people obviously have strong personal beliefs about religion and spirituality in general, but please remember that we aren't all meant to be exactly alike. I know this is a tough one, but hang in there.

When I first started letterboarding, I talked about God and my friend Jesus, a lot. Mom and Dad were blown away. My teacher wasn't though, as she said it's quite common among autistics that can finally communicate after years of silence. And it happens with teachers of all different spiritual backgrounds and beliefs, not just my teacher. There could be another whole book on this topic alone! Anyway, I had to refrain from sharing too much at once because I didn't want to overwhelm Mom and Dad. It drove Mom nuts when I told her she wasn't ready yet to hear everything from me. I revealed myself gradually over the first two years of my communicating this way and I still give them little surprises just to keep life interesting.

Please don't judge your friend as psychotic if they have views different than yours; there's no need to schedule a doctor's appointment for medication! Their views may differ from yours because their lives are different than yours.

Hint 3

You may not choose to see some things we do as "spiritual."

Many associate "spiritual" with only "religion," but there are two definitions: "relating to or affecting the human spirit or soul as opposed to material or physical things," and "relating to religion or religious belief." So, don't fear the word "spiritual."

I've heard so many people who work with autists and other people with special gifts, say things like, "I always feel so uplifted after I work with Joe" (fill in the blank with the name of any specially-gifted person), or "he always seems to know just what I need" (a hug, a hand on a place on your body that hurts, etc.). Ha! Do you think those are coincidences? Our energy can affect people on a very deep and personal level. The deeper the effect (come on, let us affect you!), the more spiritual the experience. Some may just think it's "cool" or something, but it's much deeper than that.

I've also had many people write to me for words of comfort and encouragement. I send them a note and they respond by saying things like, "Your words affected me so deeply. How did you know what to say?" or "Your words really touched my soul." My favorite is, "Wow,

I never would have looked at it that way."

We see life through a different lens than you do. Through it, our insights can be completely different than yours. And remember that many of us are professional meditators and in those meditative states, we have access to tons of information. Whew! Wild, huh? I just said it! It's been bottled up inside me for 15 years. But hey, you read the title of this book before you bought it, so if you knew all its contents already, I'd have to go back and change the title! Plus, thinking of us through a clearer lens of truth will change your relationships with your special friends, and perhaps, even give you more peace on your journey.

Hint 4

Teachers can come in subtle packages.

I am a sneaky type of teacher, as are my fellow autists. Our lessons are mostly spiritual in nature because they require the learners to go places they may not have chosen; places within themselves. There are millions of examples of this. I'll mention a few here and then continue with more in the *Idea 8* section of this book.

Let's say Mom asks me to do something like take out the recycling. There may be three bags to take out but I only take one of them on my first trip. When I return, she suggests I take one in each hand to save time. I make some autistic sound of refusal, or even say the word "no" if I can, but Mom pushes her time-saving, step-conserving agenda on me once again, "Honey, why don't you want to use both hands and take out one sack in each?" I just continue on my one-bagged quest. I feel and hear Mom's deep breath. Was it that of frustration? If so, why? Unless the big, cool recycling truck is just around the corner, I fail to see the urgency. To insist we do things exactly as you do, is a common cause of parental and caregiver frustration toward us. I call it "red energy." Well, it's not red until it becomes really serious, but it's mucky, to say the least. Mom dug a bit deeper into her "why," regarding things like this, Now she says, "Whatev'. It's just a suggestion." No energy shift from her anymore regarding these types of things.

This type of learning is of a spiritual nature because it affects Mom's human spirit. She doesn't have to experience frustration, or that pang inside her tummy, from little things like this anymore. But if I wasn't committed to teaching (and getting my steps in), she may not access the "whatev'" attitude and be able to apply it to other parts of her life as easily. Do you get my drift here with spiritual teaching?

Let's take a very pertinent teenage autism example, hormones and aggression. What the heck kind of spiritual lesson could possibly come out of this? First, let me say that when hormone surges hit, they can totally take over us, especially when combined with OCD. If we turn aggressive, it is never intentional. When you naturally go into "fight or flight" mode, your adrenaline challenges mine to an olympic race. My adrenaline is already at full speed before

Mom's even thinks of going there, so I have a slight advantage I'm afraid. Now, if Mom recognizes that and just couldn't change the environment during my "rev-up" stage, she has learned to diffuse me with a sense of calm that she musters from within. I know that spiritual lesson has been the most difficult for both my mom and dad, but the point is, they learned. I promise that we don't volunteer to teach this tragic, difficult, advanced-level course, nor would we choose to have loving students attend this class, but it's this darn mind-body connection thing that can be a monster inside of us. When I "go there," and Mom chooses to smile at me even as I show her my fierce, grit-teeth distorted face of hormonal rage, I feel the love pour out of her eyes as they lock intensly with mine. I am happy to say that most of the time, the beast has recently learned to melt like the Wicked Witch of the West. When fear used to overtake her, that was a different story. Mom's spiritual lessons from this type of thing, as well as mine, span a multitude of miles and directions and have been acquired from many sources. I'll let her tell you more in her part of the book. If this topic doesn't contain "human-spirit" or "soul" depth, (ie: spirituality), then I don't know what could.

IDEA 6

Pressure

Trying to become someone we're not
meant to be is a lot of pressure
for us to bear.

IDEA:
Trying to become someone we're not meant to be is a lot of pressure for us to bear.

MY MAIN POINT
Live and let live!

MY TAKE
Why must we all conform, lest we get labeled "off" or "weird?"

MY EVIDENCE
People sometimes do not take too kindly to others when they don't understand them, or in our case when others (neurotypical) are observing us and all the "weird" things we do. There's a tendency to wonder "why is this guy not like me?" We can read you like a book, by the way, and the pressure that we can feel from such thoughts or "side-eyes" (when people look at us to see but don't want to turn their head in an obvious manner) can have detrimental effects on our confidence. I encourage you to reflect on this. We all feel pressure to conform, I know it's not just me, right?

Hint 1

Treat others how you want to be treated.

If there was any cliche' phrase to live by, I support this one as a bumper sticker. In all seriousness, the hint here is a simple one, yet easier said than done. You are only human, but don't forget - so are we.

Hint 2

When we need to let energy out of our bodies in harmless ways, let us – with grace, when possible.

I have these loud sounds escaping lately... it's energy. I can't even begin to spell the sound for you, but just know that you don't hear it too often, unless you live with something that sounds like a combination of a Bigfoot and a Howler Letter from Harry Potter. My sound is a bit happier than that, but still probably wouldn't be appreciated at a live concert in the middle of a Mozart symphony.

I was on the treadmill at the gym yesterday and my sounds were a-flyin'. Mom was next to me on her treadmill with a big smile on her face. I might add that none of the other gym patrons even looked my way. I think that was a "first" in public. I guess the gym is a place people are used to hearing grunts and sounds coming from each other. The most helpful thing though, was that Mom was still proud of me and not embarrassed.

If we're going to a play or concert or something, we don't want to be yelling or interrupting the performance any more than you want us to! You can help us with this by just talking with us about the etiquette prior to the performance. We may need to do jumping jacks in the hallway or outside of the theater prior to entering.

Hint 3

Therapies, sure, take us to some but don't become a "therapy mad-scientist!" H2O will never turn into aluminum!

Your attitude toward and your reasons for the therapies in the first place, are important. That may sound weird, but it's true. If you have the intention to make us act, behave or be like your friend's kid, just know that we feel the pressure and it's like you're telling us you don't like who we are at the moment. However, there is a different energy from you if your intention is solely to make our lives more comfortable, fun or a bit easier. But if you forget that we're not here to emulate your friend's kid, that's when the pressure comes for us. We don't want to disappoint those we love.

Remember that we're kids who like to play or people who deserve to "just be" at times during our day, too. Also, our *play* may not look like yours, nor our *relaxation* either.

Hint 4

Talking may not be our "thing."

I know that one of the most important desires of parents is that their autistic child be able to speak. This desire is so strong sometimes, that it becomes an obsession. So much so, that parents may miss out on other accomplishments their child is making, right before their eyes. It makes me sad when I hear Mom pointing this out to parents because speech is only one of a plethora of challenges we deal with each day of our lives. Making gains in other areas may be more important to us but I know speech is of utmost importance to many of you.

You see for me, in my early days I wanted to focus on feeling good in my body, being able to walk on a path in nature without tripping and learning how to run. Now, finding a sense of calm in this life is a priority, especially during these puberty-ridden teen years. I'm not saying that speech wouldn't make communicating more convenient, but I am suggesting that other forms of communication may be easier for us at different times in our lives. It just depends what's going on in our lives and how challenging our other issues happen to be. Then we prioritize. Please know that for you to prioritize for us if far less effective.

I know what you're thinking, "I'm the parent (teacher, caregiver, etc.) and you're the kid. You can't possibly know what's best for you. I need to take charge here and help you with your well-being and your future." In some regards, yes, but not in as many as you'd think. We'll each show you in our own way, what our priorities are. For example, I used to love to read books with Mom, Dad, my grandmas and grand-pas, and my TeamTeo members. Being read to as a kid was so important to me for a bunch of reasons that had to do with my priorities at that time. I was showing that I was interested in learning to read, that I liked new information and that I enjoyed listening to stories so I could feel calm inside. Being able to focus on a story lets my brain take a well-deserved break from life's stressors. Just be aware of "auditory overload." Be sure you change the volume and/or tone of your voice throughout the book to keep it inter-esting and to keep our auditory system engaged without getting overloaded.

If you help us focus on our priorities and make gains with them, then we can feel triumphant and more motivated to move on to our next one. We'll tend to show mutual respect by working on yours, too. Notice and acknowledge all the accomplishments your autistic friend is mak-ing. Look for them! We make them every day and most go unacknowledged by therapists and parents. They range from longer attention spans, more non-verbal communication, increased coordination, trying new food, being more flexible, to more smiles in a day, and everything in between! Our accomplishments can be your treasure hunts! Happy hunting!

IDEA 7

Limitations Are Imposed

We are handicapped only by the
limitations imposed upon us
by others.

IDEA:
We are handicapped only by the limitations imposed upon us by others.

MY MAIN POINT

Our autism challenges do not define who we are or who we may become.

MY TAKE

Without being taught, how would anyone learn anything?

MY EVIDENCE

Opportunity, opportunity, opportunity! That's all we really need to succeed, learn and thrive. I hear that some of my colleagues go to school, then come home and watch Youtube videos for hours. Or they're in a Day Program of sorts, then they go home to their group home and watch TV until they go to bed. And worse yet, if it's a house full of non-verbal autistics, the shows they're watching are often cartoons or Sesame Street. Opportunities have to be given to us because initiation is challenging for autistics. I've heard the phrase, "you create your own opportunities," but that's tough when one must rely on others for help with this issue.

Can you imagine if the shoe was on the other foot? If I was in yours and you were in mine? What would your life be like? What if you were never given the opportunity to learn how to drive? Let's make that really serious and say that you were making brownies and your mate or housemate had used all but one of the eggs. You thought there were four eggs, but he/she insists on putting the shell remnants back in the carton after cracking and using them, so you thought you had plenty for your brownie recipe. How would you finish those nummy brownies that you promised your beautiful children? Oh, and did I mention, you live out in the country and have no neighbor from whom to borrow an egg? I bet you would be wishing that some-one had taught you to drive at some point in your life!

Well, now you may see the seriousness of what I am saying. I work out at a gym now. I do cardio, free-weights and weight machines. If Mom and Diane (my wonderful physical therapist/Masgutova friend) had never introduced me to the treadmill, trusted that I could learn it and then helped me do it by starting slowly and staying right there with me, I wouldn't be running on it now at 7mph and keeping a steady walking pace of at least 4 mph for 30-40 minutes! Mom couldn't run at that pace with me outside right now, so the treadmill is my pace-horse, so to speak. I rely on Mom for enough other things, anyway. Now that I'm 15 years old and my body is whacko, these workouts and the opportunity to lift weights have been my saving grace! That's another whole book, too.

Exercise Sonnet

By Matteo Musso

Shall I compare thee to a singing kid?
Thy body remembers the feeling strong.
To want you is not enough, oh feeling.
Thou hast required commitment from me.
Thou hast touched my cardiac system now.
Daily shall I attend thee, Exercise.
For you bear gifts of rejuvenation.
Walking daily and Lifting heavy things
Oh, body of Mine these gifts art for Thee.
Added joy Thou bringst , oh my Exercise.
Really effective results shall be mine.
I willst deliver mine body for you.
Exercise, exercise where for art thou?
Later today thou shallt mine be again.

Education and access to practical, stimulating information is vital to nurturing our intelligence and stimulating our brain's capabilities. When I began communicating with my letterboard at age 11 and a half, Mom asked me what my favorite subject was to study. Since we home-school, we could focus on that which was interesting to me. My response, "I don't know yet, I need an education." I needed exposure because until that point, my intelligence hadn't been challenged or fed. Again, if people assume things just because we're non-verbal or have other challenges of autism, and they don't see the point in educating us.

I am in Boy Scouts and now have so many Merit Badges. I'm blessed that Mom works so hard at being a Scout, too. She attends the meetings and participates in the activities and campouts so that I can participate. She constantly educates the guys, leaders and other parents about my way of life and makes sure I can do things with friends.

Let's talk "skills" for a minute – if left alone with a pencil and paper and told to draw something "for fun," I'd draw a house or stick figure. But if guided and actually taught how to draw or paint, I can be a pretty good artist.

Music is amazing. It takes me to beautiful places in my mind, especially when I hear it live. Whether it's the San Francisco Symphony, the Luther College choirs, band or orchestra, a musical performance of the Lion King or Les Miserable, or hearing Bette Midler, Andre Bocelli or Marc Cohn in concert, I love them all. Mom's taken me to these concerts and many more. They affect my emotions, inspire my attention, tickle my neurological system with their frequencies and nourish my soul. And playing music myself on piano, guitar, drums and assorted other fun instruments, really gets my brain going!

Opportunities – there's an instrument for everyone, no matter your motor skill level!

Hint 1

Just offer a variety of opportunities
to your autistic friend.

Don't necessarily ask them what they want
to learn or do, because we don't really know yet
– we don't know what the options are.

Be excited when you present the idea and
you'll get immediate buy-in, even if we don't
know what we're getting into!

Hint 2

If you don't feel confident or skilled
in a wide variety of things or you're
short on time, put a team together!

You don't have to do it all. In fact, variety for
us is a good thing. We like to be around other
people's energy, too. It expands us.

Here are some places Mom has found great people to share their skills and passions with me:

- Local community college
- Church
- Word of mouth
- Boy Scouts
- Yoga studio
- The gym
- Tutoring groups
- Local businesses (ex: the Lawrence Livermore Lab
  is in our town, so it's a great resource for scientists)

Hint 3

Take us to concerts, plays, etc.

I know we may have vocal issues or other "bodily action issues" which may prevent you from venturing to these types of activities with us, but please go anyway! If you begin with community concerts (outside, high schools, community orchestras and plays, etc.), people are used to having families attend. Believe me, little kids can be louder and more disruptive than us sometimes! Prepare us ahead of time for the event by showing a picture of the theater, talking about the performance and the etiquette of the event. That's really important.

Hint 4

If you do take us to these places, please leave your embarrassment gene at home.

Just KNOW that we will handle ourselves the best we are able. If you fear the potential "Martian sound" that could escape from your autistic friend, guess what's for sure going to happen – a Martian sound IS going to escape from your autistic friend! It just is. I promise you. You are actually planting that seed in us with your fear. I don't mean to add pressure to you, but it's the way it is. But just think, if you are calm and know things will be fine and you have confidence in this, guess what will happen – things will be fine! Isn't that cool! But remember, you can't fake it.

Hint 5

Buy Boy Scout Merit Badge books online and do them with your autistic friend.

You don't even have to join a troop if you don't want to or if it's not possible, but you can still have fun learning and doing all the cool stuff. They're really good guides for educating us about lots of fun activities (camping, canoeing, art, music, astronomy, weather, first aid, etc.) and even if you aren't able to DO all of those activities, you can watch someone doing them on Youtube or something.

Hint 6

We are happy household helpers!

I get to help our family run our house! Yes, I said, "get to." You heard it right. I am so happy that I am a contributing member of my family. I don't think many of us would enjoy just "taking" from you or others our entire lives. Humans, in general I believe, thrive on feelings of accomplishment. Also, please assume we can do any activities with help, practice and training. Some of us may take longer and need more practice, but we are capable. Are you capable of teaching us? I know you are. Love is a strong educator.

Mom started me with folding the laundry. I didn't know it was considered a "chore" by some, until just recently. We were visiting our friend Anne (out of state), and we surprised her by doing her laundry while she was out for the day. I won't disclose the exact number of loads we did but I learned that she doesn't favor washing towels too much. I think she can go at least six months without doing a load of towels while maintaining her household cleanliness quotient! Don't buy Anne towels for Christmas!

Folding clothes with Mom was always a geometry lesson and magic trick all rolled into one fun, bonding activity! A bath towel changes from a large rectangle into a square and back into a rectangle again. Washcloths are squares with many geometric options...triangle, rectangle, smaller square or you can even roll it so it becomes a cylinder. In our house, it depends where the washcloth is stored. Our guest bathroom gets the cylinders but the master bathroom gets the small squares. Did you need to know that? Anyway, seeing a pair of jeans turn into a small rectangle is just plain fun to watch. Transformation right before your eyes!

I also get to:
- Empty the garbage
- Take out the recycling
- Empty the dishwasher
- Make my bed
- Sort my dirty laundry
- Use the washing machine and dryer
- Fold and hang up my laundry
- Open cans with the can opener
- Go grocery shopping with Mom and Dad
- Carry in the grocery bags and put the groceries away

- Take the garbage and recycling bins
   to the street on Wednesdays
- Make my own smoothie and
   sandwiches

I'm into science experiments lately. The other day with Sara, I wanted to see if an ice cube would melt faster in regular water or sparkling water. (I won't tell you how it turned out, try it!) Mom said that later today, we'll do an experiment to see which takes longer for me to do – take out the garbage or take out the recycling. Stay tuned. (Haha, Mom. Don't think I don't know what you did here!).

Anyway, FEED US AND WE WILL EAT! Make it a smorgasbord, please!

IDEA 8

Assume Intelligence

Assume intelligence, please.

IDEA:
Assume intelligence, please.

MY MAIN POINT

Education needs to be offered to everyone.

MY TAKE

Everyone should get an age-appropriate education even if they move around and wiggle a lot, make silly sounds, don't look at you in the eyes, can't communicate with spoken words or express to YOU what they know and comprehend.

MY EVIDENCE

In my experience, this is not happening for most of the autistic people in the world, or even here at home in the United States. Based mostly on our speech skills and bodily movements, judgements are made and off to the special education class we go. Which level depends mostly on speech. Are you a high-functioning, mild-to-moderate or a severe "case" of autism? These labels, I've decided, have more to do with *society's ability to interact with and understand us rather than our cognitive abilities or intelligence.*

I think if society didn't associate speech and bodily movements with intellect, there would be more age-appropriate education going on in special education classrooms, and teachers would be rewarded for their unique and creative ways of teaching us. I've heard of a small handful of schools which are doing this, but I'm afraid they are anomalies, not the norm. I feel a change coming though, as more truths are shared (by silent ones themselves) about what's really going on inside the silent autistic. I don't believe society wants to hold us back for any reason. I just know there have been some big misunderstandings and misguided assumptions.

A lot happens when you assume our intelligence and educate us, whether our bodies may or may not be able to show you what we know. I'll list a few things that happen here, but again, there's another whole book on just this subject alone!

- Your relationship with your autistic friend instantly changes
- Respect flies back and forth between you.
- Our lives are enhanced
- Our days become exciting
- Our intellectual neurons fire up and new connections are made
- Hope that we'll get to lead fulfilling lives is ignited or renewed
- The prognosis of living a life of total dependency and boredom disintegrates

- We better understand the world around
  us and thus, we better understand
  the people around us
- You talk to us totally differently
- You include us in conversations and ask
  us for our agreement or disagreement

Hint 1

Look for our gifts and focus on them.

We'll make them known through our obsessions. If someone is fascinated with pictures of bridges, then maybe they're natural engineers. Get them in with mentors who build cool things or let them build things themselves (with your help, if necessary). You know, like they used to have, "Take your kid to work" days? Find an engineer who loves to share what he/she does. Mom does this with scientists around here. A nice chemist from our church came over and spent an afternoon doing electricity potato experiments with me.

If your child or friend loves getting into gooey stuff, maybe they're a multimedia artist! Hire an art teacher. Gianna is mine and she ROCKS! Banging on the piano keys shows an interest in creating sounds and in cause-and-effect things. I LOVED cause and effect as a kid! I guess that's why I like science.

Hint 2

We will need exposure to a variety
of things and an overall education,
just like everyone else.

I really touched on that earlier, so I won't repeat myself except to say that once you choose to open this Pandora's Box of sorts, the world is as much our oyster as it is to anyone else on this Earth. OPEN-SESAME!

Hint 3

Read age-appropriate materials to us.

Read books, stories and current events that are age-appropriate for us, not babyish. After the first reading of a book, it has the potential to become a stim or habit. It could even grow into an obsession and inspire OCD. If you encourage us to have you read the same book to us over and over, ("Oh, he loves this book so much. We read it every morning and every night!"), you are helping to create these issues. We can handle this repetitive department by ourselves, thanks. No help needed to come up with stims or repeated activities to do. Remember, we're the experts in those areas (haha). If you do read favorites multiple times, enjoy mixing up the time of day you read it, the voice inflections and use the book in various ways (like noticing how the words relate to the picture, count how many e's are used on a page and sneakily work our eye-tracking muscles, etc.) Mom used to act out Llama Llama Red Pajama and we'd laugh so hard! As I got older, acting it out even while sitting on the couch helped me read out loud with voice inflections.

Chapter books like Harry Potter, enable me to understand and actively listen to my friends at Boy Scouts as they engage in debates or conversations about latest "hot" books or current events. That's why it's important to keep us up to date on what's happening in the world, too.

Otherwise, eavesdropping on conversations is sure boring! We like to be "in the know," too.

Oh, teach us to read line by line using our finger as a pointer. This may take lots of "hand over hand" practice, but it will help greatly! Then we'll be able to enjoy reading on our own someday. Please know that we are probably able to read to ourselves with this method, even if we can't read out loud. That goes back to that over-reliance on our speaking skills (causing you to misunderstand what we know), that so many of you have.

Hint 4

If you assume our intelligence, so will others!

You are suddenly a leader and elevated to a position of power to change the world! Seriously, I'm not kidding! As it turns out, many famous people who brought society some of its greatest inventions were on the autism spectrum. If you're a parent, a teacher/therapist, or someone who is around autistics a lot, others look to you to see how to "treat" us. What will you teach them? What will they be emulating if they observe and learn from you?

I think I can point (speak) for most non-speakers, that we'd much prefer you err on the side of assuming our cognitive abilities too much, rather than not enough!

IDEA 9

Your Energy

Your energy affects us more
than anything else.

IDEA:
Your energy affects us more than anything else.

MY MAIN POINT

You can run, but you can't hide!

MY TAKE

Your true heart, inner thoughts and attitude toward us and in general, cannot be masked with fake smiles or "appropriate" words.

MY EVIDENCE

Turn believing into knowing and say goodbye to stress, doubt and worry. Why is that important? Well, first of all, we want you to stick around with us. Living long and healthy lives is a gift from God but I know we each have to play our part in this. If your energy is high-strung and we aren't able to "shield" ourselves from it, your energy enters our core, sending shocks of electricity through our bodies. OK, I can't speak for your autistic friend, but this is what it's like for me. And *what if* your friend has the same experience? One thing I ask you to keep in mind as you read this book, is that there's as much of a chance *that this is* the experience of your autistic friend, as there is a chance that it *isn't*.

So, I understand it is hard to see yourself turning believing into knowing, but today is the best time to start.

I made the following statement for my very first Top 10 List and used it to blow my parents away at the beginning of my letterboarding. "Autism is not a disorder, but rather, a spiritual energy." Are you still there? You haven't closed the book, have you? Have you ever met someone who's said, "I just love working with autistic people. It's so rewarding," or "I don't know what it is but I feel so good when I'm around them," etc. They are the ones who are letting that energy flow back and forth between us. We give as much as we receive, but all too often, the "receivers" aren't open to catch the football!

We are extremely sensitive people (in case you haven't noticed) in varying ways. We may have auditory or visual sensitivities, tactile or kinesthetic ones, too. Maybe we don't like to wear clothes because our skin is ultra-sensitive. Maybe we wear headphones to dampen loud noises like vacuuming or traffic. Maybe we cry at the drop of a hat or when you leave the house. Maybe we explode when the schedule changes or you drive home a different way from Safeway. We are sensitive beings and most of it has to do with our neurological systems. But keep in mind that we are emotionally sensitive, too. Many don't choose to believe that because we're off in "our own world" sometimes, so it is assumed that we're numb to conversations and actions that are going on around us. But here's the thing, we don't have to see, feel, touch or hear you. We can sense you! I'm just not going to keep that in me anymore, WE CAN SENSE YOU!

Mom would often stand outside my therapy room, whether we were at home or in a therapist's office, and try to listen to what's going on inside. She didn't come in therapy sessions very often because she said that I acted so differently if she was around. She didn't want to disturb anything. I was laughing inside so hard! She thought that just because she stood on the other side of a two inch piece of wood, I wouldn't know she was there. I knew it all along because I could sense her. In fact, it would have probably been less distracting if she'd had just come on in, because I was so entertained by it. But Mom thought she was doing me a favor because she did spend about five years or so being a stressed out mom. I always felt bad about that because I knew it all stemmed from my needs and special way of life that she wasn't really prepared for. But this was also an opportunity for me to teach her (and Dad) so much about themselves.

Getting them to officially register for my class took a while, but then one day, when I was eight years old, they sat at the desk in the front of my classroom. "Where did that come from?" I asked myself and God. They had been learning through the SonRise Program, how important and powerful their emotional choices actually were and how they affected me...and them. Boom! They became my star students and received honorary doctorates from Teo-U in less than three years!

Gone were "embarrassing" trips to the grocery store, in fact, gone was embarrassing anything!

They changed their energy toward me, my bodily actions, my sounds, my stimming (repeated activities like stacking blocks and knocking them over for hours), my, my, my – everything! It was truly a miracle.

Hint 1

Go to SonRise training!

Or at least read the books. They're entertaining and full of ideas. Mom would read them out loud to me and keep me in the loop about what they were doing. They were getting my "buy-in," which is actually important and affected both me and them!

Hint 2

Choose to let go of things that clog your "happiness pipeline."

Once you decide to make this a priority, your perspectives change and different priorities emerge. As I mentioned earlier about therapies (how the energy behind the reasons you take us to them makes all the difference), if the priority becomes our comfort and our relationship as opposed to making us neurotypical, it's a different journey on which we embark. You'll get the "buy-in" more from your child/friend.

Mom tends to often focus on a big concept, rather than on a single action or incident.

By this, I mean that she'll take something like a negative statement sent by a group against the way I communicate and roll it into a huge thing that will affect the rest of my life and that of so many other non-speaking autistics. It's fine to care about my future and the lives of others, but each time she shares her views with someone about this subject, her energy changes. Her heart rate goes up. Then she hangs up the phone, turns to me with a smile and wants to do an RPM lesson. "Sure Mom, like I can really concentrate when your energy is up." Until she figures out how to retell the story without her heart rate increasing, it will continue to affect our learning time together. She's working on it because she knows this.

So, it doesn't take her long to realize it and we take a break from the lesson to discuss her phone call. I know what was said anyway, so let's talk about it instead of burying it. You can do this with your child/friend even if they have no way of communicating with words yet. Just have a one-way conversation and say things like, "I know you get what I'm saying here. I wish I had a way of hearing what you'd say back to me. I bet it would be some wise thing like, "blah blah blah." Fill in our response with something you think your child might say, if you're assuming their intellect, comprehension of a situation and that they're your most wise confidant. Try it, see what happens! Remember, let them walk around if they want and they don't have to acknowledge you in any traditional way.

Hint 3

What you feed, grows.

Mom consciously knows that every time she retells the story, she feeds it. When you feed something, it gets stronger, right? This is the same concept here. It doesn't matter if it's a lion, a kid or a belief. Will you feed your beliefs pure, organic foods? Or will you choose pesticide-laden polluted stuff that once resembled food, but was destroyed by an outside source to the point of it being unrecognizable and unbeneficial?

If you have an image of your autistic friend or child leading a sad, lonely and isolated life, you are feeding that concept and that's the food we absorb into our system, too. You don't know that's how we feel. It might be the way you imagine how we'd feel, but again, that's only based on what you're seeing with your eyes and interpreting through your own life experiences.

If you choose to see an autistic person's repetitive actions (the calming ones like rocking or block-stacking, not the OCD stressful type) as bad or dangerous to his mental health, then that's what you're feeding. You'll then feel rushed to "extinguish the behavior," and you become that "therapy mad-scientist" we discussed earlier. See how this all fits together in my life? It may be this way in your friend's life, too.

In the words of Princess Elsa in the movie Frozen, "Let it go, Let it go!"

Hint 4

Inner Peace and Meditation.

Finding that sense of inner peace is a quest we go on as humans, whether we realize it or not. Some actively pursue it by seeing a counselor for talk therapy, using pharmaceuticals, talking to friends, doing yoga and meditating. The latter two are gaining wider acceptance, thank God, because they are so important and only do good for the mind and body. There are no yoga side effects. No, you won't start hallucinating by doing downward-facing-dog pose. Meditation consists of producing images in your head that are soothing to your soul and visually guiding energy throughout your body. By doing this, you remove stuck energy and the good-feeling energy can flow easily throughout your body. We create roadblocks with our emotions, especially fear, anger and frustration.

Now consider combining what you know about autism with the previous sentence. Talk about fear, anger and frustration? Try walking a day in our shoes! Do you really think we couldn't possibly benefit from yoga and meditation?

Now, how many of you are thinking, "My kid couldn't sit still long enough to meditate." I have another secret to reveal - they've been meditating their entire life! Many of you may have an image of a monk sitting on the floor with his legs crossed saying, "Oumm." Or a cool-looking person living in Berkeley, California, wearing flowy, drawstring pants, a tank top, a tattoo and nose ring, standing on one foot with her hands up in the air all day. But there's more than one or two ways to do it. When I meditate, I'm not always silent. Remember, energy escapes out of my mouth when it's good and ready, so that's how good I am at concentrating! I can be meditating while sounding like a turkey or martian. I also stare off sometimes and yes, I can go to my own world - but isn't that just meditating? If you're doing a guided meditation and listening to someone describe a beach scene with soft waves crashing and a light breeze in the sunshine, aren't you also in your own world? This I know for sure - you're not at a stressful workplace or driving in Bay Area traffic! You're in a world you created to find that inner peace.

BAM!!! So are we! But our personal meditation time is not respected like yours is. Someone is often saying that it's bad for us to stare off and "be in our own world" like that, then we get "redirected." We also get dinged points for our lack of "interactive attention span" or too much "stimming" (our repetitive behaviors that can serve as another form of meditation, too). I'm not saying that you should let us sit and meditate all day long because we too, have things to accomplish in this life, and unfortunately, meditation is considered a luxury in our society. But giving us the flexibility in our schedules to meditate when we really need to, would be very helpful and appreciated. Meditation is also an activity you can do as a family. Just don't expect every member to experience it the same way.

If your autist needs to run around a bit and you want to sit on the floor with your legs crossed as you listen to a recorded guided meditation, go for it! Live and let live. Mom comes into my room each morning and plays my grounding meditation, The Roots of Light, that Master Danadoost made just for me. I bet he'll put it up on his website if you want to use it (www.ehealing.org). Then, at the end of the day, after I'm tucked in bed with my heavy blanket and body pillow, she plays another one called "Sheets of Light." This one really can clear the stuck energy of the day. It helps me relax and go to sleep. Sometimes Mom lays down next to me (she doesn't get a heavy blanket though) and meditates with me. That can be even more powerful as we collectively experience the healing. I'm dealing with teenager stuff right now so my anxiety is higher than it used to be. I'll be happy when this is over, by the way!

So, I hope you'll consider meditation as a way of helping your autist find inner peace. Even if they can't say "thank you" specifically for it, I'll say it here for them.

IDEA 10

Befriend a Person With Autism

Befriending a person with autism
will definitely change your life.

IDEA:
Befriending a person with autism
will definitely change your life.

MY MAIN POINT

You are in charge of your transformation.

MY TAKE

Some people aren't interested at all in changing themselves. They'd prefer that others do the changing and conform to them. Well, I can't say I blame them because change can be hard. Look who you're talking to here. Autistics are constantly encouraged and dare I say, forced to change and conform to society's ways of "normality."

MY EVIDENCE

"Quiet hands - flapping isn't socially acceptable."
"Shhh - those noises sound silly."
"Sit in the chair during class. Standing and
    pacing is disruptive to others."
"Look at me when I speak to you. Show me
    some respect, please."
"Hug Aunt Sally even though you've never
    met before. It's what we do in this family."

I could go on, but you get my drift.

As a friend of mine, you get to choose how my way of existing will impact your way of existing. Whether you think it will or not, it will. I promise.

Will you learn how uncomfortable you get around people that differ from you?

Will you learn the true power that empathy has over judgment?

Will you see that you might not be as patient as you thought you were?

Will you notice how often you conform to society even against your intuition?

Will you notice how often you allow the thoughts and opinions of others to override your own and shake your confidence?

Or will you choose, "none of the above." You may not be in the mood.

I say this with a chuckle because I know we're not always in the mood to acknowledge or even notice these things.

According to the feedback I've received over the past three years as I've been publicly speaking, I think the biggest way my friends have changed is that their eyes have been opened to seeing life through a lens so vastly different from theirs and they let it remain open with others in their lives. We can have varying opinions, habits and ways of dealing with life's challenges, yet still love one another and respect our differences - not judge them.

Hint 1

Open your door. Gifts can't be passed through one that's closed.

When you know all things contribute to your journey and your learnings, and that they are from God/Universe (or the name you call the Higher Power) with a loving purpose, you start searching for the good in each situation. Keep in mind that sometimes it might be buried and harder to see right away.

Autism is a perfect example. We may be a different type of kid than you thought you were going to be raising, surprise! Are there challenges and hard days? Yes. But there are beautiful things that come from raising us and the more you choose to see them, the more the gifts will keep coming; and I mean for both or all parties involved.

Attitudes shift and emotions get felt on the deepest levels. You get to rejoice at victories that others take for granted. For example, "Hey, he just let me hug him for the first time!" or "Hey, he just jumped with both feet!" or "It was amazing...his hands actually came up and protected his face when he tripped this time!" Old friends may be lost but are replaced with those of deep character. Patience is acquired or increased, nurturing becomes natural, priorities change and you get a love shared deeper than most humans get to experience. From those who care for us, that love is selfless. From us to you, that love is patient, kind, enduring and grateful. If you close your door because things go differently than you had planned, you won't get to unwrap these divine presents chosen especially for you.

What the heck! Go ahead and take that door off its hinge entirely. This way you won't be tempted to slam it when things get rough! And don't worry, you live in a safe neighborhood.

Hint 2

Realize that just because it's the way
it has always been, that doesn't mean
it's the way it could, should or will
be in the future.

One thing I love about my mom is that she questions each "no" she's given. I've watched and listened to her do this my whole life. She says there have got to be options, then usually thinks them up herself. We can easily get into ruts and just accept what someone tells us, but that tends to be pretty limiting. It also prohibits our creativity from getting its daily exercise and squashes our intuition. If a voice in your head or a feeling in your body occurs, that's a sign to listen up! Your intuition is sharing the truth with you.

Once again, here's autism to bust up paradigms. One example is the intelligence and creativity that lies mostly undiscovered in autists, especially non-speaking ones. Psychology has had it wrong all these years, giving autists an IQ based on tests that are impossible for us to take. They had tunnel vision when telling my parents when I was seven years old, that I was functioning at the level of an 18 month old baby. I just had to go to my "zen" place when hearing Mom and Dad talk about this after an IEP meeting at school. The testers were so wrong, but I couldn't tell them.

So, now that many autists are finding creative ways to communicate to the world, things are slowly starting to change. But for me and my autistic colleagues, change can't come fast enough. Special Education classrooms are often just daycare for autistic kids and provide minimal educational stimulation. This is because we can't prove to the teachers or our parents what we know or comprehend. But now that so many autists can show their true colors, let's change the old, archaic ways of the Special Ed classroom. Let's just teach age-appropriate material and assume competence in the students even if they can't prove what they know. The information is going in, I promise. This is a perfect example of my HINT 2! Just because it's always been that way doesn't mean it should continue.

Another example is how you may do things habitually for your kids, that they are perfectly capable of doing if the skill is taught by a patient teacher. I've been emptying the dishwasher now for a couple of years. I'm also obsessed with clearing plates, cups and silverware once someone is done eating. I set them down on the counter next to the kitchen sink. (I'll tell you a funny, creative story about that in a minute). Although it can pose a bit of a problem on an airplane when we travel, like when I need a wrapper thrown away but we haven't reached 10,000 feet yet. But for the most part, people like and appreciate it. Sometimes OCD can come in handy and be productive, I guess.

Anyway, just the other day Mom said, "Now if I can just teach you how to rinse the dishes and load them in the dishwasher, we'd really have something." So, guess what I'm learning now? Where some people may cringe or complain about "having" to do this, I've adopted the attitude of my dear friend, Dick Wedge, who reminds me about this from Heaven - that I get to do it. "You don't have to, you get to," he always said to his family. I truly see participating in household things as fun because it means that Mom and Dad know I'm capable of being a productive member of the family. I know other autists feel this way, too.

Mom is a fun autism mom because she'll step outside her "box" to help include my idiosyncrasies in society or life in general. She also sneaks in "teaching moments" to those closeby.

Here is an example:

A couple of weeks ago, we attended a Court of Honor for my Boy Scout troop. It's an evening of food and fun. Guests come and we get recognized for our achievements over the past six months, like merit badges, rank advancements, etc. We always begin with dinner. As some people finished their dinners, my OCD kicked in and

I felt the urge to clear plates once again. As Mom watched my anxiety building across the room, from her table to mine, I saw her walk up to the microphone. You won't believe what she did! She announced to the group that I'd be happy to clear any plates that were ready to be disposed of and that if anyone would like their plate cleared, they should raise their hand. Well, as you might imagine, I was thrilled! An entire room filled with paper plates, cups and plastic utensils, ready to be properly disposed of - by me. It was Heaven on Earth, I must say. I was the happiest star-ranked bus boy this side of the Mississippi!

We usually don't clear the plates at a Court of Honor; everyone busses their own. But since I was in my mood, Mom made it happen and turned a potentially stressful situation into a soothing experience, even for me, with a special added extra for the guests at our Court of Honor. Just because it's never been done before, didn't mean it couldn't be done that night! That's what I mean by my Hint 2.

Here's another one:

How many of you get really happy while at the grocery store? Do you just get giddy there doing your shopping? Well, Mom and I were shopping in the produce section one day and she asked me to go by myself to the other end of it and get some organic kale. She remained way down by the bananas (we're working on my independence). Anyway, I was happy to try and do this myself and was excited that Mom asked me to do it. So, I was basically skipping through the store to the kale. I passed a man and woman who were rummaging for the perfect tomatoes when I came skipping by them, making my happy "martian" sounds. They're a very high-pitched "dig-uh, dig-uh, dig-uh," sort of sound. As you can imagine, I caught them off guard and they quickly turned and stared at me. As I hear Mom retell this story, she noticed their glaring stares in contrast to my gleeful happiness regarding my kale mission. I felt their judgemental energy. Mom knew this and just couldn't help herself. She walked over to them and said, "Don't you wish getting some kale made you that excited and happy? We could all be so lucky, right?" The couple's facial expression and energy changed immediately and they replied to Mom, "Yes. If we could all be so lucky!" Bam. Lesson taught and received.

True, people don't often skip to the kale section, but it doesn't mean you can't!

Hint 3

Open your heart honestly to us.

Tell us what's going on and include us in your emotional process. Do you have a friend you try to share things with but who keeps interrupting with their own story or problem instead of listening to yours? We're the best listeners in the world and we're right here for you. Involve us!

We're professional listeners; and remember we're listening even if we're not sitting down and staring at you in the eye. If you choose to share intimate things with us like emotions, challenges, victories in your day or your thought process on a particular situation, you'll find that some remarkable things happen. Your relationship with your child or special friend will grow deeper and more intense because your energy will have shifted to knowing that we understand what you're saying and feeling. That can be huge for some people who may not have heard this secret of autism. It's not their fault because they've probably been misinformed from those who have taught them about autism - who also haven't heard this information yet.

There's a sense of satisfaction and emotional release, too, when you share with us. We can take your honesty any day and process it. We can help release energy that's not helping you, so it can be transformed. This may sound a bit strange if you are new to this idea of energy and its power, but it's true. I've heard and felt these changes occur within my Team Teo members over the years. They could show up to play with me during my SonRise program feeling sad or stressed, but then after our hour together, they'd leave refreshed. They'd often thank me for the session. It's funny how Mom would thank them for coming, but they had already secretly or out loud, thanked me for letting them. That's when I knew that things were going to start changing for me; peeps were catching on to a gift of autism - "silent emotional counselor." We counsel with something more powerful than talk-therapy; we use pure love energy.

Another example are my friends, Anne and Jodi. They often call or write to Mom saying, "Can't wait to see you guys. I need a dose of Teo." I guess that means that I'm in the pharmaceutical business (haha).

I said before that we can take your honesty any day and process it. What is most difficult is when you try to hide your true selves from us because that means that you don't understand us, know who we are and our capabilities. Just because you haven't done this in the past, doesn't mean you can't do it today and everyday in the future.

IDEA 11

Leading by Example

We lead by example.

IDEA:
We lead by example.

MY MAIN POINT

Leading by exposing you to our challenges and showing society what changes need to happen to secure a safe, healthy, happy, loving world, is the mission of many autists, whether they know it or not.

MY TAKE

The world was created beautiful and pure by God, but man's free will upset the balance that was perfect. Now we are getting sick and leading challenging lives. To quote that singer, "We've paved paradise and put up a parking lot." Many issues are being created within everyone's bodies. We (autists) just show some of the ramifications more outwardly so the world can see, learn to care and hopefully choose to act in a way that will reclaim the Earth's purity and balance, as well as reduce human suffering.

MY EVIDENCE

If you notice the things that challenge us or things we are attracted to, you'll see what I mean.

Hint 1

Allergies and Food

Many of us are allergic to different foods or at least have an intolerance. We do much better with organic food that's free from toxins. That's us reminding you that current farming practices use chemicals that harm the human bodily vessels. God provided the Earth with soil that was pure and clean, but humans messed with it. The reactions you may see in us include: diminished speech, inattentiveness, erratic' bodily movements, histamine or anaphylactic responses, more "martian sounds" escaping from our mouths, skin redness, upset tummies we can't tell you about, constipation, intestinal challenges and the list goes on. You'll notice so many NT kids with nut allergies, eczema, etc. We're all singing the same tune with visible bodily reactions to an ever increasing polluted world. Clean up our air, water and food supply, please!

Some foods make us go nuts, hurts our tummies, some of it actually heats our brains (or at least, doesn't put out the fires that get started from neurotransmitter signals not reaching their destination in our brain due to those heavy metal blockages). But there are foods that really help. Give us a banana and see if we calm down a bit. Please feed us glucose (best is fruit) every 1.5 hours! Our organs need it - especially our brains. That's what they burn for fuel.

Check out the Medical Medium protocol. Mom and I have been following a guy by the name of Anthony William, the Medical Medium (www.medicalmedium.com). He talks a lot about how food affects us. Ever since eating as he suggests, I feel so much better. I'll ask Mom to go in to this a bit more in her section on the following pages. Since cutting out the preservatives, gluten, eggs, dairy, corn, canola oil and most refined sugar, I'm a new guy on the inside. I know that all the processed food we eat in this society is making us sick, whether you feel it now or won't until later. We're supposed to eat fresh stuff that's not in a bag or a box.

Hint 2

Keep it simple.

Simplicity - we are content with simplicity. I think we show this more when we are young and before electronics really enter the picture. A favorite game of mine was tossing rocks in the stream. I would have done it for hours if Mom and Dad had let me. It cost nothing and you couldn't wrap it, yet it was always my favorite gift. Simply blowing bubbles and chasing them in the breeze was another favorite. Stacking blocks and knocking them over and lining up my match-box cars just right were also thrills of mine. They weren't fancy, expensive store-bought items. The best gifts were activities that calmed me.

But even more beautiful was that I had someone who loved me, joining me in activities that they wouldn't necessarily choose to do themselves or even fully comprehend. The true meaning of "the gift of self." So, maybe you can save millions of dollars if you stop buying us toys just because the neurotypical kids like them. Watch us - notice what we like to do if given a free minute in our day. Does your child get a free minute or two each day? I didn't get many until Mom realized, through SonRise training, that it was OK if I had some. If I didn't, how would she and Dad ever learn what I like to do? I hereby give you parents permission to sit down and enjoy a glass of wine or tea, guilt-free! Just observe your child and smile, knowing that this is a gift you just gave him or her. Then when you get bored, come down to the floor and join us, but be sure to bring your own matchbox cars or blocks to stack!

Hint 3

Patience.

We are amazing with this virtue. You have no idea. When so much is trapped within us and we're so misunderstood, the amount of patience it takes to just live each day would overwhelm even the most practiced monk. That's one of the most needed virtues in the world today and here we (autists) come in droves, entering the world and requiring it from everyone! In the words of one of my favorite poets and singer/songwriters, Marc Cohn, "Dig Down Deep. We gotta Dig Down Deep."

Hint 4

Sensitive Sensory Systems

Does the world really need to be so loud and shocking? It seems that NTs need more and more sensory stimulation for thrills or to get their point across. This is curious to me because I find that the quieter I am as I spell, or the softer I say my words after spelling them, the harder people listen and the more they concentrate.

The movie theaters - really? Does the volume need to be so loud that it vibrates your body in order to be a good one? If I didn't wear noise-cancelling headsets when I go to the theater, I think I'd be dead!

During my presentations people often ask if they should clap out loud for me or just wave their hands in the air to show their appreciation. I often tell them that I wish the world could learn the musical word "crescendo." It means, "to get gradually louder." I enjoy the clapping and after the initial second or two, I'm fine. But I cover my ears for those seconds because sudden loud sounds are shocking to my body. It can feel like a lightning bolt going through me. But the gradual increase of sound is fine. That's why dogs that bark are not my favorite - they are unreliable and don't know how to crescendo, that's for sure!

Or what about when you have conversations

with each other? Oof-da! The political ones sure get loud fast! Try something – lower your volume as your friend's increases and see what happens. Implement this strategy with your autists, too, as they escalate from anxiety.

Sometimes we can't look at you and listen to you at the same time, even though that seems to be so important to society. It sure is to teachers, therapists and parents. But for us, it can be too much information to process at one time, so if we can't do what you ask, just pick one of those. Say, "Hey Teo, I need to tell you something," then see what your child or student does. I guarantee they're hearing and understanding you, even if it doesn't look that way on the outside. Maybe our message is, "Stop multitasking so much. You're driving yourself crazy and not doing any of the tasks to your greatest potential."

Hint 5

Energy.

We are energy experts. We've got Monster's Inc. beat hands down in the energy production department! We're proficient in both the production and consumption of energy - of both yours and our own. We're also expert readers of energy that's around us. If you're sad, we know it. Frustrated? We feel it. Tired? We can tell. Distracted? We will follow your lead. Mom knew this to some degree intuitively, but what she misunderstood was that my power of detection was more developed than her skill of covering up her true emotions. The mouth would often speak a little white lie in an effort to comfort me or perhaps, convince herself that all was well. I get that, but all along I dreamed of being able to say, "Mom, you can be honest with me. Talk to me and share your true heart. I will understand." And I say now, "I feel it anyway. Honor me with the truth." This creates depth in a relationship. So if you're looking to deepen your relationship with an autist, I highly suggest this approach.

If you're a therapist or teacher reading this book, what I'm about to say obviously doesn't refer to you. If you didn't want to increase your true understanding of us, or if you didn't care about us, you wouldn't be reading it. Your energy feels different to us than that of the other kind of teacher, therapist or doctor. We are drawn to yours but many professionals have entered the autism world because it's become such a big buck industry. We can sniff out those who are in it for profit first, then to perhaps help us. Watch your child around people - we are barometers of intention. Everything we do or ways we act are forms of communication.

If your energy is grounded, hopeful and positive, you've trapped us! You're like Willy Wonka's chocolate factory - we won't want to leave. We don't expect this all of the time because we know life isn't like that. So don't read this and freak out, please! We are all emotional beings. If you're sad or frustrated sometimes, you will be our teachers. How you deal with the ups and downs of life will help us learn how to handle ours.

THE END

20/20 Vision

The time has come to say goodbye. Hi-ho, hi-ho, it's off to the gym I go! I hope you have enjoyed my writing and thoughts but even more, I hope there was a nugget or two that you'll take away and blend into your life. If you do, then my heart will sing.

A parting poem for you, my dear readers:

20/20 Vision

When love arrives in special ways,
  it can be surprising.
Life can change from man-made plans
  to worldly compromising.

Unwrap the gifts given you from God
  and try to understand,
Each one of us has come to you,
  our purposes are grand.

Find out what purpose we have for you,
  why'd we burst into your life?
Are you going to cherish our time amidst
  the toils and strife?

I know we challenge and are unique,
  God made us perfectly formed,
To be who we were meant to be.
  like you were, too – I'm informed.

Together we'll grow and share some tears
and we'll share happiness, too.
We'll laugh and love and grow inside
in ways you never knew.

We'll feel more deeply, discover uniquely
things most misunderstand.
People will arrive into our lives to love
and lend a hand.

So do not fret, welcome us instead.
We'll take you on some rides,
To places you didn't know exist
that focus on our insides.

'Cuz the outer shell is just a vessel
that houses our own soul,
Playing tricks on us with visual lies
designed to help man grow.

Then, the people gained vision of another
sort that does not require eyes, and
saw beauty through their new lenses.

May your vision be 20/20 as you see
the inside of an autist.

Love, Matteo

FROM MOM

Some things I've learned that deepen my
relationship with Matteo, nurture his needs and
challenges, strengthen his gifts and help him
experience life to its fullest.

My husband and I have been on quite a learning curve these past three years since Matteo started communicating his deep thoughts via his letterboard. Well, we've been eating "humble pie" for years now with no end in sight. You know how sometimes it's hard to say you're sorry or that you were wrong? Let me tell you that it gets easier with practice!

My husband and I always knew our son was smart, assumed he could understand what we said to him and that the possibilities for his future were limitless. I've realized how often I said those things out loud to family and friends but never really knew the depth of what I was saying. When Teo began to share his deep, personal insights and thoughts with us, we were blown away – to say the least. To know your child is "smart" is one thing, but to really see what that means is another. Having to hire a calculus tutor for him at age 11 ½ to challenge Matteo in math was shocking enough, but integrating math with physics just because Matteo loved it, was not anywhere on my "smart" radar.

Prior to RPM, the stick figures he'd draw or that house he was asked to copy independently, (square + triangle + rectangle), would be celebrated. They don't hold a candle to what he is doing now, creating beautiful watercolor paintings and multimedia "happiness" art with help from an angelic, skilled art teacher named Gianna. Matteo's art is now welcomed by the public in the form of greeting cards or wall art.

I tell people that Matteo understood everything we said the whole time, but that really is nothing compared to the depth of inspired thought and perspective he shares with us on a daily basis. Out of all his gifts, his use of the english language completely blew us away the most. To say Teo "understood" what we were saying is like saying that Picasso was good at paint-by-number. Matteo expresses himself and shares his point of view most effectively through his poetry and creative writing. He teaches with analogies, expresses his deep thoughts through verse and inspires others through honest, heartfelt truth and active suggestions. He doesn't just say something to you; he gives suggestions and step-by-step instructions how to actually accomplish it.

Imagine an 11 year old kid who already figured out his mission in life! Two months after Matteo started open-ended communication on his letterboard, he said that he wanted to be "a voice for the silent ones," write a book to spread the truth about autism and start a company selling coffee mugs with inspiring sayings on them. Teo wanted to bring a smile to people every day. I'm 54 years old and still refining my own mission and trying to understand my reason for being.

Through unexpected blessings, I was able to leave an industry in which I had established my career and begin homeschooling Matteo. This allowed me to focus on his needs and help him with his mission. We have had several opportunities to speak in public about this crazy autism turns, ups and downs, laughter and tears and tons of personal growth. This journey has been filled with incredible, but completely unexpected experiences. Had you told me three years ago that this was going to be my life, I might have given you a nice smile and nodded my head, while thinking to myself, "She's nuts. She obviously has no idea what my day-to-day real life is about."

Matteo wrote this book as a compilation of the top ten lists we hand out at talks. I have included my own revelations which have been effective for me in relating to my son and the other kids I have worked with on this journey. Every day of my life is filled with opportunity after opportunity to learn and grow. I don't always feel like learning and growing to tell the truth, but the lessons seem to keep-a-comin' anyway.

I hope that you will find time for yourself, take some deep breaths and read the following pages with an open mind. Whatever you decide, I hope you can embrace this autism journey you are on and just remember, we are in this together!

Namaste!
Annette

IDEA 1

Choose

The autism journey will
be what you *choose*
it to be.

I am starting out with a "bang!" and in my opinion, the most powerful idea that I will share. I realize that choosing to be happy has become a cliche', but I have found it to be critical! Why? Because it has given me some power back. When we received the formal news that Matteo was autistic, both my husband and I felt completely out of control and suddenly not confident about anything anymore. We thought we were parents who had most of the important stuff figured out for our son; his education, opportunities we'd provide for him during his childhood, etc. But when he transformed right into autism before our eyes, everything changed. We no longer knew what to do, what to expect or where to turn for help.

Very often I find myself saying, "If I knew then what I know now." Then I catch myself, because I wouldn't be where I am right at this moment. If you are a parent new to the autism community and have a child who has been recently diagnosed with autism, I am thrilled to save you some major time! More importantly, I hope to save you some real emotional agony and self-induced torture on the way.

So, think back for a moment about the time you received your child's diagnosis. What was said to you by the doctor, psychologist or whom-ever delivered the news? What did their face look like and how did their voice sound? Maybe you're one of the blessed few who received the news differently than I did. From what I have seen though, most parents got what I got; "I'm sorry, but Matteo has autism." The choice of words, somber voice and sorrowful facial expression used in the delivery of the diagnosis were etched in my memory for a long time. "But don't worry, they're finding amazing ways to help kids these days."

"He may even someday be able to have some sort of job and live on his own in a group home. It will take a lot of work on your part, but it will all work out." I left the psychologist's office that day with a bag full of brochures containing hundreds of therapist's phone numbers and supplement ideas of all varieties, none of which I ever opened. I was completely overwhelmed and shell shocked!

Whether your experience was similar or different, I'd like you to take a minute right now and erase it from your mind. Let's replace it with this alternate scenario:

The doctor/psychologist comes out holding his clipboard, looks at you with a big smile and says, "Wow, congratulations, your child is autistic! You are among the luckiest parents on this Earth. The journey on which you are about to embark will drastically change your life for the better. You get to grow and learn in ways that are unimaginable to you right now. There will be a lot of amazing, skilled, knowledgeable, loving people who will help you and quickly become very special in your lives. Your "family" will expand and the love you will feel from others who understand what you are going through will be overwhelming. New relationships will be fostered, older friendships and family ties will strengthen and others you encounter on this journey will offer unique ideas and philosophies for you to consider. I can't tell you exactly who, what and when – but it's all coming your way. But I do have a word of caution for you; relationships will change and support will come from unexpected places. For various reasons, people from whom you were expecting unwavering support may not be able to provide it. You won't always understand why." I would have truly appreciated a fair warning about all that. But now I can tell you that I've never in my life encountered such loving, supportive, uplifting people as those I have met through therapies, camps, autism conferences and on our speaking tours. Many have become extended family members and I have our son to thank for introducing us. Imagine that!

When Matteo and I spoke at the Mayo Clinic in Rochester, Minnesota, we went out of our way to explain how important the delivery of the diagnosis is to the parents and how it seriously sets the stage for the life of the child. It is my goal to make a difference in that area. Can you imagine the turn of events had you left the office experiencing the positive scenario above? This may be hard for you process but tears may have been replaced with smiles, fear replaced with hope and excitement and guilt may have been replaced with confidence. Whatever your current situation, perhaps you can take this opportunity to begin anew. Approach your autism journey with the curiosity of a child instead of the fear of the unknown. Had I been offered that option and taken it, my life would have had a different "bounce" to it. The energy with which

I approached research on therapies and acquiring services for my son would have been completely different.

Hint 1

You get to see the future through your OWN eyes.

A professional simply cannot have the same vision for your child as you do. You are the parent. If it's raining outside and you had a picnic or party planned, you may choose to be disappointed. But that same rain may be a God-send to a farmer during a California drought. But, they are reacting to the same raindrops. That's my point. We get to choose what we see.

Hint 2

There's always something good that comes out of each situation in our lives. Sometimes we just have to look harder to see it.

Here's a quick example from yesterday, I swear! My husband, son and I were driving to the northern California coast to stay at a friend's house. We had our three bikes on our bike rack. Two are "pedal-assist" bikes that are heavy and not cheap! Even with our extra bungee cords, "just to be sure," one of the bikes was suddenly , being dragged behind our car as we cruised down the freeway with Teo doing his Word Search in the back seat. While Mark and I contemplated how to secure the bike, I was concerned for our safety because the cars were whizzing by so fast and the shoulder was all too narrow. I was also fearful that Teo would open his car door to complete his ritual of saying, "Mom, I finished it" after each page he completes. And he was sitting behind the driver's seat which opened to the freeway! I verbally told Teo what was happening and to keep his seatbelt on with the door closed. I also suggested that this was a good time for him to practice turning the page on his own and showing me a whole bunch of pages at once when I got back in the car.

An important side note here: Don't say "DON'T" to kids or someone with autism. Had I said, "Don't get out of the car!" It is common for kids and autistics to focus on what was said after the "don't." Matteo told me this on numerous occasions. He mentioned that there's often a "lag time" between the start of my sentence and when he realizes that I'm speaking to him. Then it takes more time to process what was said. By the time that all happens, the "Don't" is long gone and he's left with "get out of the car." Interesting, huh? I'm so grateful I had that bit of knowledge under my belt in this dangerous situation!

Anyway, when Mark and I finally got back in the car and were driving down the highway again with our heart rates doubled, we each got to decide how to view the situation. We could choose to be so upset about the bike being ruined and our bike riding vacation plans as a family were 'toast' (and I get that!), but we also had the choice to focus on the fact that we were all safe.

Are both choices "natural?" Will one choice feel better than the other in our bodies? Will one be more emotionally satisfying? That differs from person to person. There are times when each emotion is beneficial and that's my point. I'm not here to say which one was best for my husband to pick and which was best for me. It depended on our experience of the situation. I was so concerned about everyone's safety that guess where I chose to go in my head? My poor husband. He was obviously discouraged but had to listen to me repeat, "Thank God we're all safe!" No matter what he said, that was my response. I couldn't help myself.

Then guess what, we got more practice because it happened again! Twenty miles later, the bike was dragging again! We couldn't put it in the car because there wasn't any room. As it was, Teo had a space barely big enough for his body. We didn't know what to do! We strapped it on again and took the first exit off the freeway.

I won't leave you hanging here. We googled the nearest e-bike shop, drove a slow six miles into Berkeley and dropped off the bike with a guy who told me on the phone, "I can fix anything you bring me." I loved the confidence! It made me think about the relief that a perfect stranger can provide sometimes. His confidence put my husband at ease and made him smile again. We were safe to continue our drive.

Hint 3

We don't teach our kids life lessons - we show them.

What's our bike story got to do with autism or the journey with my son? Everything! Because our energy affects Matteo so much that if we'd remained stressed or overly frustrated, he would have had a major meltdown. I know this for a fact because now that puberty is in our lives, he is even more sensitive to the energy of others and the environment around him. He can go from 0 to 60 in 30 seconds or less, bless his teenage heart. He saw us choose our emotions, deal with them in our own way, and then quickly arrive at our original place of peace again. Teo is sitting right here. Let me ask him what his experience was of this situation:

"I did feel the stress, especially of Mom. On the whole though, my stress was minimized because Mom handed me one of my favorite things to do, the Word Search. It kept my mind concentrated on completing a challenging task. When this is going on, it's like a safety bubble is around my emotions and I'm protected. When I finished the page and Mom and Dad were back in the car, I immediately got to practice my breathing. Have your autistic friend blow out through a straw to learn how to exhale slowly for a long time. Aim for at least 15 second exhales. I also got to watch Mom engage with her own response, process and choose. Dad did too, but I'm not sure how conscious he is of his "process." He's a natural at finding his peace and letting things go but sometimes it takes longer. Unfortunately, I get dragged into it as I learn about and refine my own process and deal with these dang hormones. Thank goodness this all took place within about 45 minutes, so I survived. This goes on every day of my life and doesn't require a broken bike as a catalyst. The concept and process is the same in each situation we encounter, since humans are such emotional beings."

IDEA 2

Imagery

Imagery is the most powerful
form of communication.

This is one of the most important ideas we can absorb as parents, in my humble opinion. When Matteo was younger, around three to 10 years old, I could tell when he was playing a Disney movie in his head and having the time of his life. Every now and then I'd catch a sound that resembled a word I would recognize, like "hahaha, Simba," or "mean Scar!" I realized how much I do this too, and in speaking with other parents, I have learned that I'm not alone. We bombard ourselves with scary visions of the future and our fear of a potential "behavior" rearing its ugly head at the worst possible times. Is the movie I'm playing in my head different from the one Teo is playing in his? Yes, quite a bit. His is innocent entertainment but mine is energetically feeding an image, idea or thought. Remember that what we feed, grows. With that in mind, I always try to be mindful of my thoughts and if I catch myself spiraling in a downward thought headed for negativity, I quickly pick a new one. It seriously helps! Just stop that negative image in its tracks! For me, they're usually based in fear.

Recognize it, evaluate it and then choose to keep it or release it. If I choose to release it, then I replace it with a new image. It gets easier the more I practice. Try it if you want, then watch what happens. What previously would have been an emotional upheaval for both of us, gets diffused right before our eyes.

Hint 1

Take a few minutes each morning
to paint the image of what you envision
for your child's future. You'll be amazed at
how you feel and how it affects your energy
and that of your autistic friend.

I see Matteo's happy face, his joy of learning, our loving interactions and peaceful
energy. I go to bed painting images of Teo as a
person in his 20's, with a sweet, smart, confident
girlfriend who understands his way of living on
this Earth and who is proud to be with him. I see
him earning a living and contributing to society
in a meaningful way that he loves and bringing
smiles to people just as he says in his mission
statement. WHY NOT? It helps me get excited
for the day and Teo feels it. I guarantee your
child does, too.

Hint 2

Every time we have a thought there's an image that coincides with it.

I have been so blessed in getting to work with a Shafaw Grand Master healer, Behrooz Danadoost, who has shed light on specifics like this. It happens so fast though, that often we don't notice it. All we are doing with this idea is becoming an artist and taking charge of the paintbrush. Who do you want composing your art and signing your name to it? You or someone else? Once I started focusing on this idea, I was amazed at how often I'd have to shake my head back and forth in an effort to erase an image that popped in there without a conscious invitation! If this happens to you, know that you can quickly replace it with a more productive and emotionally satisfying image. Why not? Listen to your intuition. You don't need a degree in psychology or medicine, a teaching credential or an ABA degree to be able to positively affect your child and his/her education and development. Having confidence in my intuition, my love and my ability to affect Teo's energy with mine, is absolutely the most important thing I have done to help my son.

IDEA 3

Limitless

Your child's future is not limited -
it's limitless.

Hint 1

A limitless view.

Our energy transforms from being desperate, sad, angry, scared or worried to hopeful, excited for the future, curious as to how we'll get there and confident that we'll be shown the next step.

Remember that setting minimal goals for your child's future will get you minimal results. Grand goals are awesome but just be careful not to put time constraints on them. That can lead to disappointment if some goal remains unreached by the arbitrarily assigned time. Let your child reach it in their own time. Society's timelines (ex: high school diploma by age 18, college when you are 18-22 years old, etc.) don't have to apply to any of us. We often just get sucked into the established belief system. But when I actually sit and analyze these things, I find myself asking, "Who says? Why?" Also, keep your eyes open for other amazing steps your child is taking because there are many that won't be on our goal list. Too often, we're so set on getting our kids to communicate with speech that we don't appreciate the motor skill improvement, the number of smiles they share with us each day, their flexibility growth or any number of other ways. they surprise us. Keeping our eyes wide open for these things is the best treasure hunt a parent could ever go on.

Hint 2

Be thankful for where you are right now
on your journey, even if it's tough.

Believe me, I KNOW what "tough" is as our
journey is not solely filled with delight. But
there is a purpose for now and it will affect later
more than you'll ever know. Having a goal for
your child's future is good but remember, you
can still be thankful for where you are right this
moment. It doesn't have to be one or the other.

A new friend of mine threw a question out
to a group of autism moms to which I belong.
She's having a tough time right now and asked,
"How can I totally accept my child right where
he is now but still have hope for his future?" It's
an understandable question when parents reach
the "end of their rope," or are so exhausted they
can't see straight. All I can do here is speak from
my own experience and the observations and
discussions I've had with so many friends who
are raising special kids. Without total acceptance
of who a child is right now, we unintentionally set barriers in front of them that can hinder
them. The way I envision it (and it helps me
stay focused), is that each judgement of right or
wrong, each interpretation of success or defeat
or whatever your particulars are, acts like a brick
pilon on your child's road to success. They are
just one more hurdle for our kids to overcome

on a pathway that's already so cluttered with obstacles. The last message I want to give Matteo is that, "I'll totally love you, I mean totally, when you stop doing this, start behaving in this manner or stop acting like that."

It's only human to love the "easily lovable" aspects in someone. That's easy. My personal challenge is to go beyond that though; to love even that which I cannot totally understand and which challenges the very core of my being and know there is purpose in it.

Accepting your child for who he is today and being totally happy with him in no way prohibits you from continuing to search for ways to help him overcome his challenges. It serves to do the opposite. It gives him self-confidence and assures him that he is loved and accepted by the most important person in his life - you. Every day and every night, I search for the amazing things Matteo has done, then I tell him why I am so proud of him. I give him specifics and let him know that I'm so happy he chose me to be his mom. Even if we've had a tough day (and we DO have them, believe me), there is always beauty to point out somewhere. Tomorrow is a new day and it can be anything we want it to be. Accepting our children exactly as they are allows them to grow in ways that will blow your mind! Acceptance is the best fertilizer.

Here's an example that happened just yesterday: We were at Teo's music therapy session with our amazing therapist, Susan Rancer, in Oakland, California. We usually end the session with Teo singing in the microphone to a song of his choice. Teo probably has perfect pitch from what we can tell, but the interesting part is that he has trouble matching his voice to the tone played on the piano. Basically, he has trouble carrying a tune. He hears it so strong in his head but doesn't have the control of his vocal chords to make the pitches match. But yesterday, he began singing, "Can't Help Falling In Love with You," by Elvis. For the first time, his pitch perfectly matched the note at the beginning of the song. I learned what a beautiful vocal tone he has! He's never really let it go at full voice before so this was exciting!

On the car ride home, I went on and on telling him what a beautiful tone his voice has. "I've accompanied lots of singers in my day and as a (former) professional musician, I'll tell you that your tone is beautiful!" He was all giggly.

This morning during his first therapy with Kim (one of our dear Masgutova MNRI therapists), he was lying on the massage table singing. I was on the phone and hadn't heard it, but Kim was shocked that he was singing so much, as he's never really done that before. After the session, he marched into the kitchen to join me, still singing and having the time of his life! I believe that since our conversation, one in which I focused on the beauty of his voice, not the imperfection of his improvisational atonal technic, he gained the confidence and pride to let it lose! And don't we all feel good when we get to let loose doing something that we love, even if we're not perfect at it? It reminds me of a saying I love, "Dance like no one's watching."

Hint 3

Examine the purpose of each goal
you have for your child.

That may sound strange, but bare with me. When Teo was little and we were just in the infancy of our autism journey, I had a different purpose for therapy and diet than I do now. Previously, it was about changing him and helping him "recover" from autism. But now, it's so he can have a healthy body, feel more in control of himself, participate in activities he wants to do and express himself freely.

By the way, I do not like the word "recover" being used with the label of "autism," but that was the word used back then in 2006 or so. It makes it sound like our kids are sick or something. They're not sick. They have gut issues, sensory processing issues, etc...but autism is not a disease or illness. The brain of an autist processes information in unique ways.

Thank God I have evolved! I know now that my son is precisely who he's supposed to be right now and I made a choice when he was eight years old, to enjoy the journey. The stressed-out therapy-laden, exhausted, bossy, crazy mother had to go. I was feeling too old too fast! Was that a sign to change things? I'm listening, I'm listening!

IDEA 4

They Hear Everything

Your child hears and remembers
everything, even if they don't
appear to be listening.

YIKES! Matteo can tell me stories from when he was a toddler. He remembers what his "transformation" into autism felt like. He tells us stories on his letterboard, but he also shows us this. Here's an example oddly enough, from yesterday...

Teo is really into karaoke right now but yesterday instead of using our karaoke machine, I was playing the piano and we were singing. I don't know what inspired me because we DO NOT still sing this type of song, but to add some humor to our day, I broke into a song from Sesame Street ("C" is for Cookie). OMG, you'd have thought the world was coming to an end! He covered his ears, started humming and then yelling in a panicked voice, "It's over, it's over!"

Of course, I stopped immediately and took deep breaths with him. I hugged him and apologized for playing that song. I had thought it would be a fun memory. Once again, I was wrong. Later, after he was calm, I got out the letterboard and asked him to tell me about that reaction. He told me that it reminded him of how scared he felt during his "transition into autism," and that this song reminded him of it. That's courtesy of the "episodic memory" that so many of our kids have, where a memory triggers an intense emotional response. The timing for this to be true is right, as we were big Sesame Street fans when he was one and two years old. His transformation occurred when he was 20 months old.

Matteo also has told me and my husband that he heard all of our conversations about money, all of our arguments about his future and what therapies to do, etc...oh man! Had we only known that going in the bedroom and talking behind closed doors made no difference in whether he heard our conversations or not. Even if I had known that he had super-sonic hearing capabilities, I'd never have guessed that he could truly comprehend the meaning of our conversations! Once again, I was wrong. So this leads to idea number 5.

IDEA 5

Assumptions

Beware of your assumptions!

Have you picked up yet that I love the phrase, "I was wrong"? I really do. I love being wrong about things I was assuming that weren't perhaps the most positive or productive. I've come to realize that assumptions I was making on this journey were made based on my life experiences, not the life of my son. Beware - assumptions can easily misguide you.

Example: If I was hanging around a group of people and no one talked directly to me, I might choose to get sad or feel left out. So, one night when I saw a group of kids at Scouts hanging out while Teo was pacing on the perimeter of their gathering area, I got a bit sad. But then at home later I asked Teo what he thought of the meeting. He replied, "Mom, I enjoyed being around their orange energy." He explained that it can be more frustrating for him if they ask him a question and he's not be able to answer verbally, than if they just treat him like one of the guys hanging out - no verbal responses necessary. Keep in mind, Boy Scouts are 11-18 year old teenagers, so they can be quite entertaining.

Hint 1

Maybe you don't have to go through the emotional upheaval after all.

I didn't have to go through that emotional upheaval inside my heart. I chose to go through it because I was assuming incorrectly, that Teo was sad that he wasn't included in the group the way I would want to be. The truth is, they were actually including him in a better way, one that was easier and more comfortable for my son. My husband keeps reminding me, "He's not you, Honey."

Hint 2

Assume Intelligence

Talk about incorrect assumptions! Yes, this is the biggest incorrect assumption that most of society makes. Teo says it so eloquently in his presentations, "Who decided that you have to be able to talk to be able to understand language?" What will it hurt to assume that your autistic friend/child is intelligent, competent and remembering what you teach? Just teach, then move on. On which side would you want people to error if the tables were turned and you were the autistic person? The side of presumed intelligence and competence, or the opposite?

I told Teo a while back that I wished I could trade places with him for just one day and experience his life. The more I thought about it though, the more scared I became. What if something happened and we couldn't switch back? I don't honestly know if I could survive - really. I don't think I'm nearly as strong as my son.

When Teo was mainstreamed in school with an aid we provided, I remember all the homework he had and how many hours we'd spend doing it each week, especially the basic 2nd grade math. Worksheet after worksheet we'd practice the same concept for weeks at a time. But back then, Teo was not communicating with the letterboard so we could only watch his body language, see his answers and interpret his comprehension as best we could. Since he wasn't giving us correct answers for two digit addition and subtraction, we assumed he didn't understand the concept; "Hey, if you have some stuff, and you add more stuff to it, you have lots more stuff." Over and over again we'd practice at the kitchen counter. He'd be staring off in the distance, making his cute little sounds and then, Boom! give the wrong answer. I guess my point is that we need to remember that the outward displays our kids show us only tell a partial story about what's going on inside them.

Our kids are anything but traditional, so I choose not to force my son into a model of education that is traditional. Square peg, round hole? Why? We can create a "hole" that our kids can fit into, complete with comfort, confidence, challenge and stimulation. They each deserve it.

IDEA 6

Communication

Your child *does* communicate.

In our society there are a few basic ways we communicate. I think we can all agree on the most commonly used: verbal language and body language. Let's take a brief look at them.

Matteo has made it clear that he has studied verbal language and how it is used in society. And frankly, he's not all that fond of it. Whereas language makes it easier to get our needs met and to say what's on our minds, Teo points out that it's also used to lie, hurt people and to pretend to be someone you're not. I think that's one of the things holding him back from speaking more. In fact, he's shared with me that he is indeed holding back for a number of reasons that I won't get into here. I admit that was a bit frustrating to hear initially, but then I remembered he'll do things in his own way, in his own time and for his own purposes, not mine. Afterall, it is his life and I trust him. It doesn't mean I will stop giving him opportunities to practice speaking, though.

For neurotypicals, body language is often more telling of the truth. Have you ever been in sales? If not, a major part of a salesperson's training is to read body language and adjust your conversation to the customer's non-verbal cues. Push a tiny bit to close the deal or back off and let them reach "the right" decision on their own? Well, I'd venture to say that our kids are not consistent body language experts and here's why: Their bodies often are not obeying their brain, so it becomes an unreliable form of communication. Matteo stresses this, so it's information directly from the horse's' mouth, or at least one of them.

Hint 1

Your child's verbal words are not necessarily reliable.

Matteo and other non-verbal people who have found a way to communicate, either through a letterboard or a computer, continually tell us that (to quote my son), "words escape uninvited." They say words that are easiest to pronounce phonetically, words they've said most often and words that have gotten a reaction out of someone. These words may not necessarily be their true thought, choice or desire. For example, Teo has said "yes" to everything most of his life. We've actually had to practice saying "no." And all along, we just thought we had the most agreeable kid in the world!

Anyway, I'm sure most of his life we've been feeding Matteo or giving him things because he replied "yes," when indeed, he didn't want it. Here's another example: "Teo, want to read Llama Llama Holiday Drama?" "Yes," he'd reply. I'd grab the book even though he was nine years old and we should have been reading Hardy Boys mysteries or something more age appropriate. Poor kid! But I thought that was really what he wanted. Even though I always knew my son was "smart," this was before I was assuming his true intelligence, which would logically tell me that he'd really prefer a different book. I can pull out that book today and use it to work on voice inflection, but we can laugh about it and be goofy.

He's comfortable with the book. He's heard my voice inflection while reading it a million times so there's no stress as we work on this specific goal. I'm not using it as an intellectually stimulating piece of literature but rather, it becomes a goofy, crazy acting class.

Hint 2

Be aware of how your child acts in situations. There's a reason for everything they do.

I mentioned earlier that the body language could be unreliable due to the inherent mind-body challenges in our kids. But that doesn't mean that we should disregard how they act in certain situations, with certain people or at school. If their actions are consistent in specific situations, then they are trying to tell us something.

I often hear of parents saying that their kids hide or have outbursts in an effort to prevent going to school. That could also be typical of NT kids for one reason or another, as I believe they do it for a specific reason, too. Do we really know what's going on at school? Nevermind the bullying which may be more obvious; what about the sensory bullying for our kids? Bright lights, noises, too many people, a visually over-stimulating classroom and being required to sit on a hard chair when their body just has to move on it's own schedule. I'm not meaning to pick on our schools here, but I am saying that many of them have not been able to make environmental accommodations that are necessary to comfort the autistic population with their overactive sensory systems. If we add in the opposite of "assuming intelligence," although unintentional, a vivid picture begins to come into focus. I may want to hide, too. Or in reality, I was such a "pleaser" growing up that I'd probably just tough it out and pretend nothing was wrong since everyone else seemed OK with the situation.

Here's another example: There was a therapist Matteo once had whose office was in a building with other professionals. Just the atmosphere and air of judgment we'd feel when we walked in to the shared lobby made Teo's anxiety flare. I know this because he's shared it with me. He can remember the past so well and can specifically tell me these things. So, I'm just sharing them with you for your consideration. Sometimes we just are so busy wanting our kids to "behave" in public, that we may be unintentionally disregarding their communications to us.

IDEA 7

Respect Your Autist

They certainly earn respect in
ways we can't imagine.

Hint 1

"Because I'm the parent and you're the child."

How many times did you hear that from your parents growing up as a kid? Or, "Because I said so." That was another favorite in my house. My parents were very loving, so it must have just been the easiest answer to give a whiny kid (my brothers, not me of course). Well, one of the biggest things I am still trying to overcome is that my son is not exactly like me. What? If I want him to do something a certain way and he wants to do it another, I have to look at why my need is so great to have things my way. He is living a totally different life than I am, full of sensory, neurological and physical challenges that I cannot even comprehend, so why is my way right and his isn't? Mine may be right for me but not right for him.

- "Wear two socks that match please."
- "Carry that computer with two hands."
- "Stop flapping your hands, Sweetie."
- "Can you pick a t-shirt that matches a bit better with those shorts?"

And for my loving OCD guy who needs to put things away in the kitchen immediately after we're done using them, "You don't have to clear that plate now. Just sit and enjoy the Big Bang, then take it to the sink later." But guess what; it's really important for him to clear his plate right away when we're home, so my husband and I have dropped our wants in cases like this, in order to let his be met. Our relaxation is different than his because if he had his plate on his lap (yes, we eat on the couch sometimes), he wouldn't be able to enjoy the show at all.

This even goes for therapy or Boy Scouts. If Teo is just too tired to go, his needs come first over mine. Even if the therapy session will cost me money anyway, it's not worth stressing out my son because I've made a commitment on his behalf at a time that was convenient for me and the therapist. I have to remember that sometimes as a parent, I have to be the flexible person I'm asking my son to be.

Hint 2

"See Johnny? Do it like him."

How many of you have taken your kids on playdates with NT kids hoping that they'd "rub off" on your child - that your child would imitate the NT child? I sure did! I'm not saying that's a bad thing to do, but I am recalling how the energy with which I approached the playdate must have hurt my son. I was basically telling him, "The way you're doing it is wrong. See Johnny over there, he's doing it right." My son enjoys life differently than I do. That was a huge revelation for me.

Hint 3

"Know always that they are
doing the best they can.

Our kids want nothing more than to please us. They're the same as any other kid in that manner. With so many professionals analyzing their weaknesses, they could easily feel like they're fighting an uphill battle.

I taught piano for many, many years in what I affectionately call my "first life." I have a double Master's degree in piano pedagogy and performance and have taught a wide variety of students in my time. For the past three year I have been giving Matteo piano lessons. Of all my students over the years, guess who is my most challenging student? Yep, my dear son. By challenging, I mean that he is challenging me, my teaching skills and creativity. For two years he couldn't tell me what the name of a note was on the staff. In fact, it's still not his greatest strength verbally. If I give him the letterboard he gets it perfect every time. But as we know, fingers need to be pressing down piano keys, not pointing to a letterboard if we want to learn how to play. Or do they? Was my previous way of teaching using the standard pedagogical approach getting in the way of me teaching my son in a way he could learn? Absolutely! I'd see Teo practicing over and over and still making the same mistakes. I'd catch my energy changing to frustration and telling him to concentrate harder. Then I'd give myself the proverbial "baseball bat to the head," and realize that he's trying so hard and absolutely doing the best he can. Sometimes it's truly divine intervention! What right do I have to judge the amount of time it should take him to accomplish a task or learn a passage? Uff-da, so much to learn.

I am happy to share that those times are rare now, but they still creep in more than I'd like. Keep practicing, Annette. You'll get it. I've realized what's really needed are more creative ways of teaching. Why is he still making that mistake? The curiosity takes over and I must leave the comfort of my box and think outside of it. The answer always comes. It's amazing. It simply cannot come when I'm frustrated, though.

I try to transfer what I've learned from teaching my son piano to other aspects of our lives together.

- He is always trying his best given his situation and circumstances (which may be invisible to me) each day.

- It's my job to be creative and think out side the box for an alternative way of teaching him. That goes for schooling, life-skills, self-help skills or anything at all.

No one ever told us this parenting thing would be easy. But when we dig deep into our creativity (and by creativity, it could mean seeking ideas from trusted outside sources, too), it helps our child and there is no greater feeling. By the way, yes, you are creative!

IDEA 8

Open Mind

Keep an open mind as you
hear about new therapies
or ideas.

Keep an open mind even if it's drastically new to you because I must say, the most effective therapies for us have been entirely new ideas for both me and my husband. I know that since ABA (Applied Behavioral Analysis) has been received as the standard in medical care for people with autism, newly diagnosed parents perceive it as the only therapy available which can affect their child's behaviors, relationship development and reduce their autism symptoms, but it's not.

Hint 1

Not all effective therapies are covered by insurance.

I'd go as far as to say that most effective therapies are NOT covered by insurance. Physical Therapy, Occupational Therapy and Speech Therapy are usually covered and could be even more effective if offered more than ½ hour per week, which is standard in many school districts. But parents beginning their autism journey don't even think to find additional private therapists as a way to increase their child's progress because they are told that what they are getting is what their child needs. I've never heard of a school saying to parents in an IEP(Individualized Education Plan) meeting, "Feel free to get additional OT from a private practitioner. We'd actually recommend it." We'd all be demanding that the school provide more then, right? And that's not going to happen. The supply isn't meeting the demand as it is, so it's a tough one.

People also flock to ABA because it is "covered," and that's a big deal financially. I get that. In fact, I was one who successfully fought my insurance company single-handed (without an attorney) to get them to pay for Matteo's ABA. At the time (2006), it was up to me to prove that it was "medically necessary" for Matteo. But what I've learned is that the majority of therapies which have helped Matteo the most on his autism journey have been private pay. I hate to say it, but it's true. And that's not fair. I'll just go ahead and say it again, that's not fair! My dream is that some day we will have an open system in which we as parents, who know our children the best, are given a sum of money equal to that which is being spent on ABA therapy, to use at our discretion. A girl can dream, right. I do know there are some people fighting for this and I'll support them all the way!

Hint 2

Scientifically proven, really?

I'll tread lightly here, but suffice it to say that as I've evolved on my autism journey, I've learned to trust my intuition more than science when it comes to autism therapies. Matteo has often said to me, "Mom, why do people want to study us so much? We're not lab rats." He's so right! Our kids are not easy to take data on, either. They're very complex people after all, not fixed entities like a number. Nothing about them is black or white. We deal with a rainbow of colors that can change minute to minute. Even in the autism therapy scientific studies, the results often rely on parental observations. When a study relies on "observations," from anybody, I feel like you're asking for trouble. We are all human and are little bundles of variables. If I had a hard day at work and my patience was short, I'd judge my son's "behaviors" more critically (and probably more negatively) that if I was having a chill, nonchalant day. Poof! There goes your reliable data. How do they know if the degree of behavior change was based on my son or on *my perception of him* on any given day? So, I'm a science skeptic when it comes to autism. I firmly believe that has worked in my favor though, as it was easier for me perhaps, to welcome approaches to autism that are not based in science but rather in people and relationships.

Hint 3

Talk to other parents.

The best information I have ever been given about autism therapies and education have come from other parents, not from schools, doctors or especially state-funded entities designed to help us. Teo calls his public presentations, "The Best Kept Secrets of Autism." Well, I could have one called, "The Best Kept Financial and Therapy Secrets of Autism." I don't know why it persists, but it does. It really comes down to who has to pay for what therapy - and it's all expensive. So, talk, talk, talk, join social groups, Facebook groups, etc., where parents share ideas about this stuff. Contact local non-profit organizations involved with autism. If they can't answer your question, they'll often have resources to help you. Find a beautiful autism story that hits home with you and contact the parents for advice. Find out how they got where they are or whatever it was that attracted them to you. What therapies did they do? What nutritional approaches did they use? If you're hungry for information, an experienced autism parent is often willing to share their journey with you.

Many of us are paving the road for the next generation of autism parents with the hope that maybe their road might be a little less bumpy and that they can be better equipped to handle the rugged terrain.

IDEA 9

Sky's the Limit

The sky's the limit for
autistic people.

As Teo said, "We are handicapped only by the limitations imposed upon us by others." To quote my dear friend Dawn Brown, in a song she wrote for her autistic son entitled, "My Autism Song" (My Beautiful Life, available for download everywhere online); "With love and acceptance, there's nothing you can't do!"

Hint 1

Remember to ask them.

Let's give our kids more opportunities to participate in our everyday lives. I am amazed in our daily life how much Matteo surprises me. For example, we've been juicing celery and cucumbers for months now. I just got a new juicer that requires our cucumbers to be sliced a particular way in order to them to fit into the slot. The other morning I asked Teo to help me by getting the cucumbers from the back refrigerator. He brought them to the kitchen, proceeded to take them out of the bag, peel the organic stickers off, wash them, put them on the cutting board and then said, "Cut the knife." I told him to go ahead and that would be very helpful. I didn't explain to him the new way they would have to be cut. But when I turned around there they were in a perfect pile, cut exactly the way they needed to be to fit in our new juicer.

How did he learn that? I never showed him..

Here's the thing; even though he was often pacing in the family room while I was chopping up the celery and cucumbers, he noticed. He notices everything, how it's done and the process. The trick is, at least in my house, I just need to remember to ask him to do more things instead of doing everything for him. He's perfectly capable of so much more than I give him the opportunity to do. And believe me, I am happy to share the household chores with someone who is so excited to do them. By the way, you can have fantastic geometry lessons folding clothes together!

Hint 2

Boy Scouts

Since we joined Boy Scouts two and a half years ago, we have never, ever been bored. There are so many outings and opportunities to be with other kids. The only problem is, being a mom in her 50s who has to (ooops, gets to!) go on all the activities with him, I feel like I hold him back sometimes. His troop tends to hike and camp a lot, so it's helping me get back into shape, but sometimes I'm just not up for the challenge. A few weekends ago I had to forgo the advanced-level 15 mile hike which included the first five or six miles ascending at a very steep incline. I'm sure Teo could've done it but I just didn't have it in me that weekend.

Anyway, he is now the rank of Star Scout and almost ready to be a Life Scout. He said he wants to soar to Eagle which would be fantastic but is completely up to him. Matteo has also been elected and re-elected three times to be the assistant chaplain for the troop. Once again, if someone would have predicted and told me three years ago that my son would be on his way to becoming an Eagle Scout, I would have dropped my jaw on the floor.

Again, giving them opportunities is what it takes.

I know there are now scout troops for kids with special needs in some areas and that is certainly an option if it's available to you. But what I did was email the leaders of the three troops in our area and told them what I was looking for in a troop. I'll share more on that in the next section.

Even if you don't actually join a troop, Boy Scout merit badge books (over 100 of them) are filled with great information and interesting opportunities and activities for education. You can get them online through the BSA website.

Hint 3

Community and the Arts

Providing opportunities to participate in the arts has proven to be extremely important to Matteo. Music, art, poetry or expressive writing of any kind is so good for the soul and provides a freedom for our kids that they do not get in therapy and school. The arts allow our kids to be free to express themselves and create from inside their hearts and minds with no risk of being "wrong." Imagine how refreshing this would be for a person who is often told to do things differently than what naturally comes to them. We have found the most special teachers to help Matteo with drums, guitar, piano, art and creative writing and it is a blessing to watch them work with him. They're out there waiting to help our kids. Maybe seeking them can become a quest for you as it did for me. For me, as far as therapy goes, what could be better than "therapy" that challenges Teo's motor skills and neurological system while nurturing his soul. Music and the arts do this.

Going to live concert events is so much fun for Teo. He wears his headphones (don't forget to bring them if you choose to go) and loves experiencing the energy of the crowd. The first concert we attended was Bette Midler (he loves "The Rose" and all her movies). We were in nosebleed seats but Teo loved it! The following week Andrea Bocelli came to town, so off we went. I'll share what Teo wrote about it:

Journal Entry
Andrea Bocelli concert

June 4, 2016
San Jose, California
The night after...

Teo: I'd like to say that looking at people last night was so fun. I enjoyed the concert so much last night.

Mom: What was your favorite part?

Teo: Much about it was best. Having a date with Mom all dressed up was special. All the singers and musicians were so talented. The choir was neat hidden back there.

The quick conversation we had
the morning of the concert:

Teo: Mom, are we going to a concert tonight?

Mom: Yes, to hear Andrea Bocelli!

Teo: Does that mean we get to go out for dinner beforehand? I'd like to take you to dinner with my allowance money.

(Needless to say – I had the most beautiful dinner of my life with my 12 year old dinner date.)

Mom: If you were a music critic, what would you say about the concert last night?

Teo: Last night I heard something extraordinary in Andrea Bocelli. Love flowed out of one of God's most beautifully created instruments - Andrea's angelic voice. A strong representation of how God's gifts can be used to transform the soul were displayed all evening. Andrea Bocelli exemplifies graciousness to God – kindness through demeanor and reverence of heart.

The note Matteo wrote about Andrea Bocelli:

As a pre-verbal autistic 12 year old boy, I admire the way this man adjusted to life, not succumbing to any limitations that blindness may present, but nurturing God's gifts in his other senses. He has reminded me to nurture my strengths while living in a society not yet equipped to totally accept autistics. Nurturing God's gifts can change world-wide perceptions, even more so when used by those who climb higher mountains.

Thank you Mr. Bocelli, for nurturing my soul with your music and inspiring me to climb to the highest mountain top singing my own song of acceptance for autistics.

God Bless you,
Matteo

I always prepare for days ahead of time if we are going to an event, on an airplane, to a festival, the dentist, etc. I find YouTube videos of similar events and play them for Matteo so he can know what to expect. This eliminates the stress of the unknown and for a guy with OCD and anxiety, this can be very helpful. He has thanked me for this preparation many times.

IDEA 10

Seek Playmates

Seek playmates and friends for
your child on the spectrum.

No, they do not enjoy being alone. They just have challenges knowing how to invite themselves into a social group, especially if they are pre-verbal. I've learned to always make it a point to pre-set the stage for success whenever I bring Teo into a new social situation. I guess that's a soft spot for me since I'm such a social person.

I'll tell you one of my most vivid childhood memories that may account for my sensitivity in this area. When I was in 2nd grade I was staying with my grandparents who lived about 1 ½ hours from my parents house. It was a big deal to be that far away for a whole week! Anyway, Grandma took me to the public swimming pool and as she sat in a chair reading her book, I was wading in the pool looking for new potential friends with whom I could play. Usually, I was pretty good at introducing myself and joining in a game with kids, but this one incident remains in my memory and it seems to be more easily accessible than others. It's a curious thing, because it isn't one of my favorites.

I swam up to a girl who looked to be about my age. I said, "Hi, I'm Annette. What's your name?" Can you believe that she actually said, "None of your business," turned around and swam off. I just froze. I don't know how long I stayed in that same position but I remember feeling like I couldn't move. I ended up crying to Grandma. We left, stopped for ice cream and headed home to get a hug from Grandpa. I recovered quickly with the loving triage I received, but that memory creeps into my mind all too often as I see my son trying to join a social group but not quite knowing how to do it. While I've had to work hard at letting the fear around that scenario go and inviting it to leave forever, it's given me incentive to come up with creative ideas regarding how I can minimize the chances of that happening to my sweet, loving son.

To be honest, for years I didn't know if socializing with peers was even important to him. I know now that he is no different from most kids in that being accepted by friends his age has its place on the self-esteem barometer. Thank God, it's not too high on Teo's but nonetheless, it's there. We've worked very hard in our family, to build Teo's self-confidence and encourage him to follow his heart. We know he can accomplish anything if given the proper support and tools. That's so important to actually do and talk about with your child, even if he does not respond back using conversational language.

Anyway, as I said, I do my best to set the stage for success when I invite Teo to try a new social situation. I don't just "show up," expecting NT kids to know how to interact with my son. Back to my Boy Scout example: When Teo told us he'd like to join Boy Scouts because Papa suggested it, I emailed three different troops in our town. I wrote quite an extensive letter to the Scoutmasters letting them know what I was looking for in an extracurricular social/learning group. I'd await the responses before scheduling a visit, if we'd go at all. I immediately received a response from the leader of the troop we ended up joining. "We'd love to meet Matteo and have him join us. Why don't you come to our next meeting." The rest is history in the making.

I've explained to the Scouts on a number of occasions, how Teo communicates, and encourage them to ask him questions and get to know him. I've also become the Disability Awareness Merit Badge counselor and teach (along with Teo) awareness to troops in the SF Bay area.

Journal Entry
February 1, 2016

That was the best boy scout meeting because I got to share who I am with my peers and they accepted me just as I am. I am happy to be me. And when I talk more, it will be even more fun.

If we invite others over to "hang out," I make sure to have games in which Teo can participate that don't require a lot of language (*Spot It, Yahtzee*, outdoor sports, swimming, trampoline tricks, etc.) Even just hanging out watching a movie with a friend or two is awesome. No words needed! I remember a friend of mine in college once saying to me as we just sat in silence for a while one night, "It's sure nice not to feel like I have to talk." A true friend can sit with you in silence. It may be a big stretch for most teenage guys to feel comfortable with that, but I still feel that it's an amazing statement and I've remembered it all these years.

Hint 1

Keep in mind that there are different ways of enjoying friends.

Your autistic loved one may not enjoy social groups the way you do. That makes sense though, because even my husband and I enjoy social events differently. Matteo has made it clear to me that sometimes he just enjoys being around "the energy" of his friends. It's as much fun for him to step aside and watch the Boy Scouts act like crazy teenagers as it would be for another person to be participating. He doesn't necessarily have to be running around and shouting like they are to be enjoying himself. He may be off to the side covering his ears, but he has a big smile on his face.

Hint 2

Prepare the social time/event with
activities appropriate for all to enjoy,
including the autist.

If Teo was six years old again and I was in
"playdate mode," I'd certainly still arrange them,
but I would speak to the parents ahead of time
and share with them Teo's challenges and also
that he enjoys social interactions differently that
their children might. I'd give examples of what
Teo loves to do for fun and encourage them to
allow their kids to join in with Teo some of the
time, giving him a chance to be the leader of
games (yes, even if his game is running in cir-
cles flapping his hands or jumping up and down
a million times). I'd set the stage for success,
rather than just get together and try to "strong-
ly encourage" Teo to always do what the other
kids are doing. Playdates can be structured so
that each child gets to be the "leader" throughout
their time together.

Hint 3

Look for social groups established in your area which focus on community service and personal growth.

These groups usually attract a special type of young person who is self-motivated and a bit more open-minded. Some examples are Boy Scouts, Young Life, 4-H, and Demolay. There may also be different home-school groups that meet to do activities. Look at Meetup groups for less formal gatherings. There's a group there for every interest under the sun! Remember though, be sure to share important informa- tion with the group on how to interact with your child. If you're meeting a Meetup group to go hiking, before you take off you could just say something like, "Hey Everyone. I'd just like to introduce myself and my son, Matteo. He's autistic and speaking isn't his primary form of communication. He's not a real conversa- tionalist, but he loves to listen to conversa- tions and he understands everything you say. I just wanted to share that with you in case you try to speak with him and he doesn't respond verbally to you. He's not being rude. Nice to meet all of you and we're happy to be here hik- ing with you today." As a side note, Matteo has expressed how being in nature has such a calm- ing effect on him. So my advice: When in doubt, go for a hike! Have fun - just get out and do stuff!

Journal Entry
July 23, 2016

Teo: Something changed today inside my head. Lots of training has paid off. Now I can handle more challenging social situations. I'm able to ground myself in this world better. Mom, I notice myself trying to have more interactions with kids now.

Mom: I noticed that today, with Zara, too.

Teo: Yes. It was easier today.

Mom: That's great! Do you know what changed?

Teo: Yes. Lots of exposure to nice, caring kids. Lots of practice is needed though.

Mom: I notice when someone says "hi" to you, you don't respond unless I prompt you. Why is that?

Teo: I don't realize I should right away. My brain realizes it but I can't get words out so fast.

Mom: What if we take the verbal pressure away and you just looked at them, smiled and waved instead. Would that work?

Teo: Yes, that's a good idea.

IDEA 11

Our Attitude

Our attitude is EVERYTHING!

Turning believing into knowing is powerful.

I've been taught that knowing is better than believing because beliefs can change when things start to go awry or they don't happen the exactly how we had planned. Does this sound familiar? "I used to believe that but I don't anymore." I am grateful to have received this message because it's made a huge difference in our lives.

Hint 1

Perspective

I've come to learn that our kids provide more perspective that we could ever imagine. I wrote this piece back in 2012 as an Autism Awareness Month message that I was asked to share at my church when we were just six years into our autism journey. I recently found this and was quite happy to reread it. Teo has been teaching me about perspective from day one, not just since communicating through his letterboard. I thought I'd share it with you...

Church Autism Awareness Message
April 2012, by Annette Musso

April 2011, I stood here and shared with you some of my adventures with my son Matteo, who has autism. Here I stand, another year older and yes, I'm going to shout this - "another year wiser!" Welcome to Autism Awareness Month, 2012.

When Matteo was diagnosed with autism 5 years ago, I'd have never guessed that I'd feel so blessed to be the one standing in front of you today talking about autism. Usually, when you walk out of the doctors office having just heard the news that your beautiful child has autism, you don't jump up and down holding the five pound bag of therapy and support group brochures, saying, "Yes, we won! We're the lucky ones – our baby is autistic!"

Well friends, through the grace of God, I'm standing in front of you embracing my son and his autism, 100%. I know you may be thinking that I've lost my mind, so we'll come back to this thought...

The CDC just released new statistics regarding the rate of autism as of this month, it was lowered from 1 in 110 children to 1 in 78, 1 in 54 boys. Autism is now considered an epidemic and is drastically affecting an entire generation of children.

I'm asked daily for my opinion about the reasons for this increase. We could deliberate for hours about the vaccine issue, environmental issues and better or different diagnosis criteria and labels being used.

Frankly, I'm not even going to go there anymore. There's no doubt that what we're doing to our environment is affecting the health of all of us, but specifically autism? I believe that the reason these special beings are coming to us is quite different.

If you read the newspapers or watch the news at all, I'm sure you agree that we're in a bit of a mess down here on Earth. Good news though, I believe God has decided to help us out by sending us angels - small, adorable, innocent little angels who will attract our attention.

Go with me for a minute here...

What if God said, "You guys don't communicate clearly or lovingly enough with each other anymore," so He sends little angels who struggle with language and challenges us to notice all the different ways we communicate.

"Your priorities are sure pretty messed up at times," so He sends little angels who don't care about the way we look, what brand of clothing we wear, how many Christmas gifts are under the tree, how powerful we are at work or how much money we have.

"You're letting the events of your daily lives stress you out, drain your energy and even depress you." So God sends us little angels who know how to block out the world and it's stress to find innocent, unobtrusive ways to comfort themselves which are harmless to others around them. They don't turn to drugs, alcohol or violence to help themselves feel better. They go into this world whenever they need to, not when given permission by someone else.

"You are so concerned about what others think that you sometimes lose your true selves and go along with the crowd, just to fit in. " So, God sends us little angels who do what they need to do to take care of themselves, despite societies labeling, negative judgements and the mocking of peers.

"You sometimes disguise your true intentions and feelings behind masks of smiles and forced laughter," so here come little angels who are radars of good intention and positive energy. Angels who know what's going on inside us at any given moment, and you can't fake it – believe me.

"You lose hope sometimes or listen to the prognosis of humans there on Earth, instead of taking your concerns and questions and placing them in My hands". So, God sends us little angels who are immediately attracted to and bond easily with those people who have found inner peace.

"You often look harder at the hole than you do at the donut." He sends us little angels who entice us to notice the many small miracles they accomplish each day. No, Matteo can't yet carry on a conversation with us, but he sat up here with all the children at our Easter service without me by his side, and he gave me a smile as he turned and walked out with his friends. That was a first, an additional Easter miracle for me!

"You're not eating right and taking care of your bodies, " so He sends us little angels who require special diets, organic, preservative-free food to relieve them of severe abdominal pain. We are forced to notice!

And finally, "You are very quick to judge each other and yourselves! " He sends us little angels who are non-judgemental and respond lovingly to those who have chosen to adopt that beautiful attitude. Only God is fit for judging.

See where I'm going here? What if this was true? Would society and us as individuals take a closer look at this epidemic? Would we get more involved? What would we learn?

Would the Aspergers child who talks over and over about the same subject transform from being annoying and odd, to an opportunity for us to practice patience and understanding?

Would a child with no language remain a "sad tragedy," or would he become an opportunity for us to realize that every part of our body is communicating our inner beliefs and the way we feel about and view our lives?

Would the "picky eater" be transformed into a living example of how we should be putting pure and nutritional food into our bodies the way God created it?

Does the child who is viewed as a troublemaker at school because he won't sit quietly at his desk and makes strange sounds at inappropriate times now become OUR teacher - because classrooms are too crowded, rooms are over stimulating and our kids aren't getting enough attention?

What if we choose to see autistic people as angels from God here to deliver very specific, loud messages?

Is autism a sad, hopeless tragedy or is it a gift? You see, what God has taught me through my son and others like him, is that autism is just the stimulus. What we chose to believe about it and thus, how we respond to it is up to me. It's up to all of us as a society.

With God's help, I've chosen to see my son as the most extraordinary gift for which I could ever ask. God gives each of us many gifts. Some are wrapped up tighter than others and are more difficult to unwrap - it's harder to actually see the gift! But you may choose to unwrap them anyway or perhaps you'll just put them in a safe place and wonder what they are and why God sent them to you.

I'm trying to spread positive messages and creative ideas about autism to this community through my non-profit organization, Creative Autism Solutions Team (CAST). This month celebrates our one year anniversary! Please visit our table in the social hall after the service to learn more!

What gifts has God given to you? Are they still wrapped up sadness, unhappiness, pity or hopelessness? Give it some thought. Maybe you'll choose to unwrap them some day and if you do, beware my friends, your lives will be forever changed! And you'll feel a happiness and peace that defies any verbal description!

Are you ready? Amen!

Hint 1

Confidence

Matteo has told me that when I'm confident in something, he feels it and he becomes confident, too. Before Matteo could tell me that on the letterboard though, I had learned it from a dear friend. I applied this concept to our RPM beginnings. When I decided to pursue RPM, I told Teo that we were going to start a new educational approach and that it will be new for both of us - we'll be learning it together. I told him I knew it was going to work because after all my research, I felt it was so right for us. Then we began, already dedicated to its success. I knew we'd be successful at it and learn to communicate with each other but I didn't know how long it would take. I was committed to the long haul and put no time limit on it. We weren't going to *try* RPM, we were going *to do* RPM. Yes, Star Wars has taught us some great lessons. To quote Yoda, "Don't try - do." When we try something, we give ourselves an "out" to give up. When we say we're doing it, we are automatically committed. Our kids feel the difference and it affects them. They will progress at their own pace. They'll learn anything we teach, but the less pressure we put on them, the quicker the success will come.

I was trying to teach Teo some science a couple of years ago. Now, I'm not a science buff at all and my memory seems to have left me half the time, so even if I read something in a science book, I could forget it before I get to teach it to him. So, I would find myself always checking to see if I said it right. My lessons were quite boring that way. I apologized to Teo for boring him and he said, "Mom, I learn better when you are more confident and really understand it." I'll never forget that. So I stick with subjects that I'm confident in and hire tutors or get volunteers for the rest. It's awesome! Or if I have to teach something I'm unfamiliar with, I'll study it harder before I teach him.

Hint 2

Prepare

So learning that my confident attitude is so important to Teo, I try to incorporate that into everyday life as well. Example: Going to a symphony concert. Teo is letting out "martian sounds" as he calls them, whenever they need to come out. It's his way or releasing energy. But martian sounds during a performance of The Messiah, especially during one of the beautiful arias, would not go over that well with the rest of the audience. So I really prep myself by visualizing the perfect scenario; our perfect concert experience over and over in my head the days before the performance. It's a great activity to do first thing in the morning with you wake up but aren't out of bed yet, and again, right before you go to sleep. I talked about it a bit earlier but it's such an important tool that I'll mention it again. Anyway, lo and behold, Teo made it through the entire performance without a hitch. Now, if you've never taken your child to a live concert before, you may not want to begin with the Messiah. Choose a shorter, noiser, family-friendly one and work your way up to the more intense classical performances if that's where you want to go. More symphonies are having "family" performances now. Theater groups are, too. I guess I don't want my fears to prevent Teo from having beautiful experiences in his life. They can happen. They just may take some extra research, planning and a bit of work on your part. The visualizing is fun and it's become a sort of "zen" thing for me.

I hope that your journey through autism is beautiful, even if some days you have to look a little harder to see it. Believe me, I had one of those days yesterday. Autistic people are truly our angels and we are so blessed to have them in our lives. May society realize what gifts they are and what we can all learn from them.

Blessings from our family to yours,

Annette

ABOUT THE AUTHOR

Matteo is a 15-year-old self proclaimed "Autist on a mission." From the first day he was able to communicate his deep, personal thoughts through his letterboard at around age 12, Matteo has been saying that he has a mission to accomplish during his lifetime. This mission is to "be a voice for the silent ones." He is proud that he has made an agreement with God to share the "truth about autism," with the hope of enlightening a society which has misunderstood this special group of people for decades and thus, bettering the lives of autistic people around the world.

Matteo travels the country as an inspirational speaker, presenting to groups of all sizes. He's a gifted poet, musician, artist and all-around sweet guy. He loves to learn about anything and everything and has a thirst for education and knowledge. Matteo also loves being a Boy Scout and in his free time, loves to swim, shoot hoops in the driveway and spend time with friends and family whenever possible. Oh yes, and his favorite pastime is eating! After all, he is a growing teenager.

Come and follow Matteo:
www.matteomusso.com

Receive a special message every Monday via Matteo's Vlog at his YouTube channel:
Matteo Musso official

Resources

www.ehealing.org
Shafaw Grand Master Healer Behrooz Danadoost
Wonderful, healing meditations you can download.

www.masgutovamethod.org
The neurological body work that helps me a lot. It
integrates primitive reflexes.

www.medicalmedium.com
Learn a whole bunch about nutrition and foods
that can really help us. You can get the recipe for
the Heavy Metal Detox Smoothie we drink everyday
and discover the power of celery juice.

www.halo-soma.org
Learn about the Rapid Prompting Method that I use
for education and communication.

www.heedrpm.com
Lenae Crandall, the RPM specialist/teacher with
whom I study. This is a great website, full of information
gathered from Lenae's experiences working with
hundreds of students all over the world.

www.matteomusso.com
Come see me!
Get on my email list to keep up with my latest news!

My YouTube Channel Vlog: *Matteo Musso Official*
Subscribe to receive a message from me every Monday!

45008352R00137

Made in the USA
Middletown, DE
13 May 2019